Sacred Presence

31-Illustrated Reflections on the Holy Spirit

Shirley Veater

Selwyn Veater

**Shirley Veater and Selwyn Veater,
with The Rev. Dr. Martha Toney**

Independently Published

Amazon/Kindle

ISBN: 9798860013698

Copyright 2023

Authors Include:
Shirley Veater, artist and author; Selwyn Veater, author and poet; and The Rev. Dr. Martha Toney, author of *Journey to Living Light* and *Journey to Daybreak*.

Holt Publishing
HoltPublishing4U@gmail.com

Additional books can be ordered on Amazon.

For book signing events email:
shirleyveater@gmail.com
martha.toney@outlook.com

DEDICATION

These words written through the unity of His Spirit
and the original art are dedicated to the Father, His
Son, Jesus, and to the Holy Spirit
sent to live in all believers.

SPECIAL THANKS

Rita Valentine Golden whose lifelong devotion to our
ministry is stellar and faithful.

Vickie Holt, publisher, editor, and friend. Without
Vickie's skill sets this book would not exist.

TABLE OF CONTENTS

OUR PRAYER BEFORE WE BEGIN

God, You love the world so richly that You sent Your
Holy Spirit to share our gladness and to comfort us
when we were in our deepest needs. For You are
closer than flesh, closer than the very breath we breathe.

We, too, have a cross to bear. We may be persecuted
for Your sake, but we will share a little glory in Your love
as we walk the earthly path that Jesus trod, strong
in the faithfulness that leads us to a cross.

So I praise the day that made Him and Jesus mine:
for all eternity, mine forevermore in His Kingdom
of holiness that never ceases,
His Kingdom that has no end.
Amen.
Selwyn

ALL PRAYERS AND

THINK ON THESE THINGS

ARE BY

SELWYN VEATER

The Annunciation

THE ANNUNCIATION

It must be an astonishing thing when an angel appears one day, uninvited, in your home.

Amazingly, Mary felt no fear when the angel Gabriel appeared before her. It is true that she was troubled over the meaning of his message—when Gabriel told her not to be afraid—but there is no evidence of fear. That lack of fear is quite surprising. Therefore, it is worth a moment for us to compare this situation with the immediately preceding one: the annunciation of John the Baptist. We are specifically told that Zechariah, a priest, was both troubled about the event and also felt fear. It might be said that this is too slight a difference, but we also read about the fact that he was struck dumb, whereas no such restriction was visited on Mary. So the Annunciation to Mary was special and her lack of fear significant. Her whole attitude of doing whatever was required of her fits very appropriately with her trust, her confidence in God, and His angel's Presence.

The village of Nazareth rolled on from day to routine day. Nothing of importance happened there. And though this was probably the most significant happening in the whole nation of Israel—or, for that matter, the world—the people noticed nothing. They laid no stone to mark His birth, no pillar to show where God had touched the world.

But Mary's lack of fear remains surprising. Perhaps her life of piety had made her more responsive to things divine; we shall never know. It would explain both her courage in the situation—and, more importantly—it might also tell us why God chose her in the first place. He does not act in random ways, but He does reward faithfulness and trust.

One of the most attractive qualities of Mary was that she just didn't realize that she had found favor with God. Humility like hers is very endearing, as well as rare. It implies a life lived in the knowledge of His will and in accordance with it.

And that resolution was greater than it first appeared. Mary not only took on the virgin birth—as wonderful as it unquestionably was—but at the same time she undertook years of motherhood to bring Him up as the man who could redeem the world. No other task has ever been so demanding, so delicate and so important. But she did the whole thing impeccably. She must have taught him ways of truth and love and the endless forgiveness He lived out in His life. His sublime character, if only at the edges, was due in good part to His mother, Mary.

Amen.

Selwyn

THINK ON THESE THINGS
God often speaks to us. Mary listened.

PRAYER

Mary, by your life of Godly devotion we saw
how we might live closer to God's will, for
our true mission is to serve a loving God.

He spoke to you through Gabriel and you
responded to each aspect of His will.
And silently you promised Him much more.

You would devote so many years of life
to raise God's Son to manhood and
to be the man who could redeem us all.

You taught Him ways of truth and love
He learned to worship and forgive,
watched you pray and remembered.

For in those lessons even we, who watch
admiringly, must ask, "Who but a mother
could teach Him love as great as His?"

You helped fit Him for His mission
here on Earth, No other task in history
has been as crucial or as sensitive as this.

And for this, all nations will call you *Blessed,*
for you magnified the Lord with all your heart.
Amen.

Advent ~ The Road to Bethlehem

ADVENT
A YOUNG JEWISH GIRL SPEAKS

"I could hardly believe my ears when my fiancé Joseph told me we had to travel the ninety-odd miles to Bethlehem to be counted in the Roman census. Our baby would be born soon. This journey was a difficult one without the added concern for an unborn baby.

"Joseph and I were chaste; this baby was no ordinary one! Let me tell you. Way back in the spring, I was kneeling at my prayers, as usual, when I heard my name, 'Hail! Mary'! I turned to look and there stood the Angel Gabriel!

" 'You are to be the Mother of God' he said. He explained when I asked him how The Holy Spirit would be the father of a baby boy, who would be Emmanuel… God with us. That was nearly nine months ago! Now I have to pack all we may need onto our donkey and set out.

"I've thought a lot about this. In scripture, the prophet Micah predicted the Messiah would be born in Bethlehem, that means *house of bread*. Oh yes, and Isaiah spoke of a virgin giving birth to a Son. Little did I know, when I read that, that I would be that chosen virgin!

"We set off for Bethlehem. What a rough and difficult road that was! Uneven, the donkey stumbled and jolted under its heavy load.

"As darkness fell, we feared we may be attacked by robbers, who lay in wait for lone travelers.

"Wild animals roamed here, too. It was winter and nights were bitterly cold. But we had great faith that all would be well, so we traveled on, trusting in God.

"I walked sometimes; we joined other travelers and exchanged greetings with them. As we got nearer to Bethlehem, lots more people were travelling there, too. I hoped and prayed we could find an inn or a lodging house where we could stay. I must confess I was feeling a little apprehensive; but we traveled on, trusting in God that all would be well."

Now let us look at our Advent. The word means "The Coming." Through its four weeks we prepare ourselves to welcome the coming of the Christ Child: Jesus at Christ-Mass, the Son of God, and Savior of the World.

We also look to prepare ourselves for the time when Christ will return to earth as He has promised.

So let us each day prepare ourselves to meet Him as we travel along the uneven roads of our lives, so that we may welcome Him just as He welcomes us.

We travel with Mary, and like Mary, we are not alone. The young Jewish girl then dedicated three decades of her life to nurturing Jesus. Let us dedicate our lives to Him and attempt to grow in grace.

Following Jesus and travelling with Him is an unending *birthing* of His life into our own.

Like Mary, with the assurance of the Holy Spirit living within us, our journey is safe and secure.

May God grant us the courage, like Mary, to carry on in faith through every difficulty. May others witness the miraculous work of the Holy Spirit in the out pouring of divine love in our hearts and lives too.
Shirley

THINK ON THESE THINGS
Advent is our Lord's invitation to His birthday.

PRAYER
God of the manger and the night, whose son I seek,
I look toward His birth, Summon me to His stable
that I may find grace where He lies in the straw.

Settle my heart in the way of perfect love as I await
His coming, that I may be ready when Your word
is made good in flesh. For it is Christ who comes
to me in the night, who enters my winter with light.

God of the long, slow journey to Bethlehem
grant me both patience and eagerness
as I long for the coming of Your dear son.
Soon You will come into my life; You will be true
beyond my expectations. You will love me more
than I understand. In the world's noise, You will be

my peace. For You bring me the peace of a child.

So, the joy begins to stir in my heart, and my
gladness grows as You come closer, for
You bring a holy light from heaven in Your birth.
Amen.

THE INCARNATION (1)

Unto us a child is born. Unto us a son is given, ...therefore also that holy thing that shall be born of thee shall be called the Son of God (Luke 1:25).

An Eternal Covenant had been made between God and the Jewish People. A Messiah would be born to save them, via the genetic line of King David. But they believed he would be like David, a mighty political King who would keep them from the ravages of earthly tyranny and slavery. But God saw that His ordinary people needed more than salvation from wicked people. He saw that His children needed salvation from sin and death. But how was this to be achieved? The only answer was for His divinity to come to earth and live as a human being.

But when Christ our Redeemer took on human flesh, He took on far more besides. He knew He would. He took on Himself our hunger and our thirst, our weakness and our weariness, our sadness, our fears, and all the other things that beset us. They were unavoidable; they were part of our human condition.

But he was not left without resource. He was also given a comforter, the Holy Spirit, Who would be with Him at His Baptism, His Temptation in the Wilderness; and, as He Himself said with Him at His reading in Nazareth. Indeed, because He had borne these things *Himself,* He was able in His Sermon on the Mount to speak with real authority of those who mourned, the meek, and the merciful, of

The Incarnation

those who were reviled and spoken of falsely, whilst He Himself hungered and thirsted after righteousness.

And at the reading in Nazareth, when He proclaimed, "The Spirit of the Lord is upon me," He told us what the Holy Spirit would help Him achieve: He would preach the gospel, heal the brokenhearted, and give recovery of sight to the blind. And those things are precisely what He did, and more. Throughout the early days of His mission here on earth—and possibly even later—the Holy Spirit was at hand to comfort and support Him. He was, after all, in one sense the Holy Spirit's son, no less the Son of God, of course, for the Holy Spirit is an essential part of the Trinity, is indeed *pure God in Himself*, and we are safe.

And, of course, death was the result of our sin. Therefore, for God to save us, He had to become one of us, and in us to strive with sin and experience death. And finally, to rise again, for the Resurrection was undoubtedly His ultimate glory here on earth. And through Him alone could God's pure bloodline be restored in us. He who had given Christ human life would also raise Him from the dead, so that for the first time in human history it would be the Spirit, not the desires of human flesh, that would become the prize of all of our lives. Union with God would be empowered by the living Spirit of God. So, the Spirit would have a cosmic mission, He would establish Christ's church on earth at Pentecost and be with us to the end of the earth. His transformative power would be available to us all. He would be with us, and in us, and throughout our beings. That same breath of the Holy Spirit that brought light into the Creation would enable us to walk with God again, in a garden in the cool of the evening.

So, thanks be to God for the miracle of the Incarnation and for the Holy Spirit, who is forever the Spirit of all Truth, our Comforter, and our Friend.

The miracle of Christ's coming to Earth to save us is far above our ability to comprehend, but we thank You for the supreme grace that was willing to take on our nature, so that we might participate in Yours. For the Incarnation was the highest example of trust. Mary trusted God to do whatever was good and right. She obeyed His will with unquestioning grace. She believed in God with all her heart. And that is a greater compliment to her than any our willing tongues could pay.

But far above the human trust of Mary and Joseph, there was a trust that is yet more wonderful, and more incredible. It is God's trusting humanity in spite of His experience with its infidelity.

Trusting *His Son* to live and die amongst us, as well as trusting all the rest of humanity was quite a giant step of trust, and it was only because they gave each other their total and mutual trust that God's great plan for our salvation could take place!

And finally, there was Mary, for in her care and devotion for her newborn son, we see her offer her great love for Him; we see her observing in herself the first and supreme commandment: thou shalt love the Lord thy God with all thy heart and with all thy soul and with

all thy mind. And in that love she carried out the first commandment of God. So let us praise Him for the incarnation and love of Christ our Redeemer and Savior, whose kingdom we now may enter, and which shall have no end.
Amen.
Selwyn

REFLECTION
Heaven stoops to earth, as helpless as a baby.

THINK ON THESE THINGS
Lord, You knew the score, but You still came; nothing could keep you from coming to us.

PRAYER
Christmas is Yours, alone, dear Lord, for
Your star lit the world's first Christmas
and Your angels sang the world's first carol.
Wise men knelt before you,
for homage is our only gift.

I pray for those who give You room at Christmas,
and those who endure the loneliness of busy streets.
for Christmas is also a parable of the homeless.
Herod's men could not find You for they

hunted You with rage and slaughter in
their minds. The way for us is easy; we
come to You only with love and adoration.

Grant me to be sanctified by Your coming
for it is Christ who comes to me in the night,
who invites me to new life in His love,
who pardons all my iniquities,
and absolves me through His grace.

Come to us at Christmas, dear Lord,
we long to receive you into our hearts.
And we ask it in the name of the child.
Amen.

THE INCARNATION (2)
THE INN KEEPER'S WIFE

"I must get this stable cleaned out, again. We're retiring from inn keeping; its hard work, and we're getting on a bit now, at our age, to be serving and keeping everything going! Our son and his wife are taking over from us, so I want to leave everything ship-shape for them, give them a good start. This stable place is so special though; I will miss coming in here to remember. Let me tell you about it:

'It was about thirty-odd years ago now. The Romans had one of their census counts—I'm sure they did it just to disrupt people's lives—it was good for business though. This couple came knocking at our door, we were packed out, our inn full to bursting! My husband sent them off, but I saw her pale face, looking so gentle and calm, her eyes pleaded as they met mine. I could see she was near her time, too, bless her, with all that noise, she looked worn out. I guessed she'd come a long way and riding on a donkey on rough roads in her condition... more than I could have done.

'Her husband looked a bit anxious, too. He seemed older than her. I looked at them again as they turned to leave, and something seemed to say I must help her; it was as though I was being prompted to do *something*, anyway. I brought them out here, made sure there was some clean straw where she could lie down. With the door closed, the animals breath would give them some warmth. Winter nights can be very cold.

Incarnation - The Light of the World is born!

'At last, we could close the inn for the night. I made sure the couple in the stable had something to eat and drink. She was curled up in the straw. I'm sure her labour had begun. How I wish now I'd stayed and helped! She was so young; but the man, Joseph, a carpenter, seemed to be coping well, and I was really exhausted, so I left them.

'I woke in the middle of the night as I heard footsteps in the yard. What on earth's going on? I peered out and saw a group of scruffy-looking men, one carrying a tiny lamb. Shepherds maybe; they usually stay out on the hills, especially at night with so many wolves about.

'The following morning, what a mess the inn was in! So much clearing up and cleaning to do. Yet I knew I must take food and drink out to the stable, too. I wondered how they'd managed last night.

'I prepared a tray and carried it out to them. I will never forget the sight that greeted me, the sweetest little baby all wrapped up in swaddling bands was lying in the animal's feeding trough on the wall, just lying there, snuggled up in the hay.

'The girl told me her name was Mary, and this was a very special baby. She was grateful for their shelter. I determined, as soon as all the travelers left, I would give them lodging in one of our rooms in the inn, where I could look after her and help her with caring for her precious baby. She would be like the daughter I longed for, but never had. I stayed quiet in a corner for a while, daydreaming as I leaned against my broomstick: I imagined the baby grew to be a sweet little toddler, good as gold!

'I listened with tears in my eyes as they named him *Jesus*. Quite a common name for such a special person. Inside, I felt he *really was a special person*. I wondered if he would be famous or known for his wonderful gifts and talents. I dreamed of his rich future. Ah, Once seen, never forgotten. I mustn't stand here daydreaming any more. I have my work waiting for me.' "

What the inn keeper's wife didn't know was that the baby she met was actually God in human flesh. God Incarnate. That baby was both Human and Divine.

What else do you know about this life that she didn't?

Earth now is linked with Heaven. Angels told those shepherds about the birth. This wasn't just a birth; it was an incarnation. The Holy Spirit was the Father of Jesus. God Himself became human, becoming part of His own creation. Almighty God, Creator of all things seen and unseen, becoming a tiny, totally helpless baby, completely dependent on Mary and Joseph. He was homeless, and at that time, shortly to become a refugee in Egypt. What an amazing story; you couldn't make it up! What a start to an earthly life, too!

This story is a turning point in the history of the world. A new covenant with God is just beginning. Time and dates begin again. The new Christian era has just begun with the sound of angels singing and the cry of a new born baby.

As we reflect on this woman's story, we see how closely the Holy Spirit was in action. He gave the inn keeper and his wife the impulse to help Mary and Joseph when they needed it most. Later the Holy Spirit gave Joseph the message to travel to Egypt, safely out of harm's way, and also gave Joseph the confidence to act on a message delivered in a dream. In all the journeys of Jesus during His earthly life and beyond, we can read about the Holy Spirit's actions: at the beginning, and remaining constant to the very end.
Shirley

REFLECTION
You brought us light from heavenly light, were heralded by a star's prophesying glow.
Shirley

THINK ON THESE THINGS
You came to us in love.
Made this the holiest night ever.

PRAYER
We kneel before you expectantly,

acknowledging your divinity at last,
subdued by your holiness, and eager
for words that will forever change us.
But we cannot linger in Your stable
as the oxen do, for outside there is work
to be done, for who should glorify You if not us.

And whose lips should sing your praises,
but our own. For we are saved by Your grace
and love and must proclaim Your glory to the world,

We are the sons of toil
for whom Your blood was later shed,
for whom You were deserted
by Your Father and Your God.

You who brought us light from light,
were heralded by a star's reassuring gleam,
leading us on to greater light.
You came as surely as shepherds,
further than wise men, Nothing
could keep You from coming to us.
Amen.

EPIPHANY
THREE WISE MEN

I begin by saying that I don't think the wise men were wise just because they saw the star. They weren't chosen by God for that reason. Anyone and everyone could see the star. But only they saw beyond the star, the greater light, and only they had the commitment and the perseverance to follow it on that long and arduous journey. Their wisdom rested not just on their perception, but also on what they were prepared to endure to come where the Christ child was. And that is a lesson for every one of us.

For what a reward they earned, kneeling before God's child, making a first church in the house, making the first worship. They offered Him their gifts of gold, frankincense and myrrh.

Probably the most famous birthday gifts ever given. But surely chosen with sadness, knowing what they foretold about His life and death.

And there is so much irony in their visit to Herod. Not only were they looking in the wrong place, (He never had much use for great wealth), but they did not see that Christmas is also a parable of the homeless and they did not understand that they must look among the poor and destitute to find Him. For it is there, among ordinary people that His heart lay.

But that is not the only irony. It was the Chief Priests and the Scribes who told Herod where the child would be born, the child who appeared to threaten Herod's very dynasty,

Epiphany

and it was the Chief Priests and the Scribes who would condemn Him in His later life. However well intended, they would be instruments of evil at His death as they unwittingly were at His birth. And innocents were slaughtered, as they always are.

So how wise were these three men, really. They arrived at the wrong **place** and certainly very late, didn't see how Herod was tricking them and had to be warned in a dream to return to their own country by another way.

But though they may not have been practical men, they really were wise in their perceptions of things that really matter, in seeing and believing in the sign that God gave them, in looking past long hardship, searching diligently for His son and worshipping Him when they did eventually find Him. They saw His majesty, and it was so much greater than anything Herod could have imagined. Greater, I think, than any of us can, either.

So let us honor those who see God's signs, willingly undergo hardships and give their time for the one greatness that makes their lives truly worthwhile. Amen.
Selwyn

THINK ON THESE THINGS
Wise men come from the East. The dawn is coming to Israel.

PRAYER

Wise men, star led, you come to Jerusalem,
seeking a God who is not your own
and yet is everybody's.

You come looking for a distant God
and find He is already here, that
the kingdom of God is among us.
Were you looking for a God of power,
to be served with subjection and fear?

You found He would serve the lowliest.
For He is always with the lowly and humble
He heals the brokenhearted and
raises up those who are cast down.

You looked in a palace rich with ornament
when He was with the animals, for He
had made them, loved them, too.

But now you will find Him easily,
deep in a loving human heart, where
He is forever cherished and adored.
Amen.

THE BAPTISM OF OUR LORD

"...but I came baptizing with water for this reason, that he might be revealed to Israel" (John 1:31).

"...Jesus loaded the burden of all of mankind's guilt upon his shoulders; he bore it down into the depth of the Jordan."
Pope Benedict xvi

The Baptism of Jesus by John the Baptist was a cosmic event in the history of the world. This galactic event in the life of our Lord took place in a prophetic location, the Jordan River. It is believed that in this location, the Israelites crossed into the promised land and had a new beginning. At this very place, the people of God were finally delivered from their past life of slavery.

John, the cousin of Jesus, was once again calling God's people to repentance from their sins. Just as the Jordan River had offered the people new life physically, the same river now offered people a new life in the Spirit. To those who came from the religious class, John would call "brood of vipers."

Many who came out to John to be Baptized from Judea and Jerusalem proved insincere in their repentance. However, from Galilee, Jesus came to John for Baptism and embodied true humility and submission to His Father. Therefore, the timing of the arrival of Jesus for Baptism is of utmost importance. It had been four hundred years since a Prophet had spoken. John the Baptist is the last of the Old Testament prophets and the forerunner of the Messiah.

The Baptism of Jesus

John did not recognize Jesus as his cousin (John 1:33). It had likely been years since Jesus and John had interacted. Actually, thirty years had passed in Jesus' life since his birth. No one knows much about Jesus' life during those thirty years. This event of Jesus' Baptism by John initiated the three years of ministry in which Jesus began his journey to the Cross. The sinless Jesus would stand with sinners at Baptism and go down with sinners in their sin for cleansing, just as he took the place of sinners on the Cross of Calvary. He who knew no sin became sin for us so that we could live as if we had never sinned through faith in his submission to His Father. Just as the Spirit was present at the world's Creation, so would the Holy Spirit make a monumental appearance at the Baptism of Jesus. The Gospel accounts describe an encounter between John and Jesus. John did not feel worthy to Baptize Jesus. John would tell Jesus that Jesus should baptize him, John.

Jesus responded: "Let it be so now; for it is proper for us in this way to fulfil all righteousness." To Jesus, it was simply the right thing to do. It was what His Father desired (Matthew 3:15). He indicated that John would baptize with water but that the one who comes after him would baptize with Spirit and fire (Luke 3:16). Two dynamic events changed the world forever. First, the Holy Spirit, present at Creation, broke through the heavens, descended, and rested on Jesus. Heaven came to Earth. Second, the voice of God spoke: "This is my Son, the Beloved, with whom I am well pleased" (Matthew 3:17). Jesus was before many witnesses anointed as Messiah. His Earthly ministry had begun.

The Dispensation of the Holy Spirit had entered Earth, and you and I are living now in this dispensation. He came in power to be with the second person of the Holy Trinity in every action that Jesus took in the three difficult years of his ministry. The Holy Spirit would empower Jesus for miracles, healing, raising the dead, and teaching Truth. The Holy Spirit would actually raise Jesus from the dead after his crucifixion. Fifty (Penta) days after his ascension, the Holy Spirit was sent to 120 disciples in the Upper Room. On Pentecost, all disciples became empowered to take the Gospel to the whole world.

The Holy Spirit communicated Jesus' Divinity to his humanity and allowed the Second person of the Trinity to be fully human and fully God. And it is the Holy Spirit given to us as a magnificent gift at Baptism who sanctifies us in our spiritual journey to enable believers to become made in the image of Christ.

It is impossible to adequately emphasize the importance of the role of the Holy Spirit in the life and ministry of Jesus. Likewise, it is impossible to make clear the multitude of ways the Holy Spirit guides believers. Only through the power of the Holy Spirit are we delivered from our sinful past and made clean. The Holy Spirit fills us with joy, power, strength, and courage to live out the calling on our lives to become children of God. Amen. Martha

THINK ON THESE THINGS
Baptize us, Jesus. We need the touch of your hands.

PRAYER AT JESUS' BAPTISM
Dear Jesus, You knew how Baptism could cleanse,
though You were already sanctified. Yet You
came to the Jordan, and to John, and to us.

For You are not a distant God, looking down
on us from above. You are with us in the water.
Divine though You are, You are one with us

The Holy Spirit descended on You from above,
coming as a dove, showing us how You came
from Heaven to earth, both pure and free.

You came for our release, now we are free.
You showed us forgiveness, bought with Your life,
rose from the water as You rose from Your tomb.

And we saw how nothing could hold You, for You
were God's mighty son, and would bring us forever to His
love and His Life if we only believed.

Lord, we believe on You.
Amen.

In the Wilderness

THE WILDERNESS
CLOUD LANDS OF DARKNESS

When the devil had finished every test, he departed from him until an opportune time (Luke 4:13*).*

Have you ever had a season of unbelievable joy only to be followed by a phase of despair and anguish? Jesus had just such an experience following his revelatory baptism in the Jordan River. What ecstasy! The Father spoke audibly "This is my beloved Son in whom I am well pleased!" The Holy Spirit descended and remained on Jesus as a sign of his covenantal consecration for ministry. All was made perfect for the Jewish Messiah to bring the Good News to the whole world. Then something very odd happened. The same Spirit who blessed Jesus at Baptism led Jesus straight away into a forty-day trial period of tremendous agony. His sunshine turned into shadowlands. What Jesus experienced in the Wilderness of the Judean Desert applies to each one of us in our wildernesses: two spirits will speak to us daily. One spirit is evil and ends in death. The other Spirit is Sacred and gives us Life. Jesus listened to the Holy Spirit who remained with him throughout his three-year ministry, his arrest, and his crucifixion and this same Spirit raised Jesus from the dead. The Spirit allowed Jesus to be tested in the wilderness to teach Jesus to hear the correct voice.

The wilderness is never fun and is always filled with enormous struggles and challenges. However, if we open our hearts to the lessons presented during these battles, and if we see the events as preparations for strength for future trials, the wastelands we endure offer enormous gifts of grace. It is exactly in these murky stages where our wills are forged and our characters are chiseled into people of marvelous material for potential greatness in the kingdom of God.

The wilderness teaches us not only how to listen to the voice of Life, but also the maneuvers of the enemy of life, Satan, or the voice of death. Here we learn that this world is not our home. Our home is Heaven. We are in a spiritual battle the whole time while here on Earth. The desert prepares us for success when faced with combat by forces that would destroy us. Cloud lands require great humility and dependence on that which we know is true.

In John's Gospel Jesus speaks of his sanctification to his disciples in the High Priestly prayer. Although Jesus was God in human flesh, he allowed himself to endure the trials of the wilderness to be an example to his followers, both then and now. To know Truth, to not be deterred from following Truth, and to hold firm in difficult places requires faith in something much greater than ourselves. In the wilderness, we learn to throw ourselves into the arms of God.

Satan tempted Jesus in every way possible by even using God's word to allure Jesus to bend to Satan's will. But

Jesus answered him with God's word and truth. Jesus rejected the schemes used against him. Interestingly, later when Jesus was faced with even greater temptation in the Garden of Gethsemane before his crucifixion, Jesus recognized the evil voice that once again tried to appeal to Jesus to abandon his destiny. Father, take this cup from me cried our Lord in his great agony; nevertheless, thy will be done. The greatest wilderness lay ahead of the Son of God. He was given the strength by that same Holy Spirit who not only remained with our Lord on the Cross but also raised Jesus from the dead. The voice of the Holy Spirit is a distinct voice most easily recognized in our greatest persecutions. May we acquire a keen ear to hear, and may we have faith that this Spirit goes with us in every dark corner and will remain with us not only in this life but will raise us too from the dead to eternal life in the world to come!

Scripture: Matthew 3:17; Mark 1:13; John 17:19

Martha

THINK ON THESE THINGS
The whole world was a wilderness, even among the Chief Priests and the religious rulers of Israel.

PRAYER

Lord Jesus, come to the wilderness in my heart
and rule until I grow like You in love,
in goodness, and in care for all my fellows.

I do not serve You well. My soul is parched with thirst
that comes in this life-sapping wilderness unless.
You're there. It craves Your water of endless life

Only You can save me from this wilderness where
doubt and disobedience flourish. I cannot pull myself
to holiness unless You grant me Your salvation.

Yet just beyond the wilderness Your waters of Life.
run pure and free and those who find them will
grow rich in grace and streams of everlasting life.

Stay with me Holy Spirit that in life and death
I may set my feet on the path You show me and
be true to you and Jesus Christ, my only Lord,
Amen.

REFLECTION

There is only one way out of the wilderness, and that is
through Jesus, our Lord.

THE SERMON ON THE MOUNT

The Sermon on the Mount towers above other sermons. It places God at the epicenter of our lives, the crux of everything. At first reading it may not seem so, but it is the essential thread that holds the sermon together and is, I believe, essential to our understanding it in full.

Our Savior begins by blessing us, perhaps it's what we might hope for from a loving God. But His blessings are lavish, they pour out upon us, the poor in spirit, those who mourn, the meek, the merciful, those who hunger and thirst after righteousness, the pure in heart, the peacemakers and the persecuted, I do not believe our Savior excludes anyone who loves Him. Indeed, He exalts us even further, we are the salt of the earth and the light of the world. So it follows that we must behave fittingly and He then tells us how. We must turn the other cheek, and go the extra mile. We must even love our enemies. Because that is precisely *how God loves us* and that is what He does. He is at the center of the whole concept.

So, this passage shows us from the very start, just how totally our Father loves us. Read it again with this in mind. He lists all our better qualities. It is almost like a lover adoring his beloved.

It is also the first authoritative statement we have about the nature of God. Our Lord tells us how we should behave toward our fellowmen because it must follow naturally from the way we behave toward God, and He is at the very

The Sermon on the Mount

center. Jesus wants us to behave toward others as God behaves toward us, and as we'd wish our fellowmen to behave toward us, because in this way we shall be acting like our Father in heaven.

So we should delight to offer the extra mile and turn the other cheek; they are Godlike actions. And when we pray or fast or give alms, we should not think about ourselves, at all; nor how we appear, but **undertake** them privately because their value lies in doing them from love of our fellows, not to increase our reputation among friends. And in this way we shall lay up for ourselves treasures in heaven, where they will not deteriorate as they would on earth.

Then He teaches us the sublime prayer that we say to this day, the Lord's Prayer. And no comment from me would be worth its space in comparison.

He counsels us not to think too much about what we will eat, drink, or wear, I suspect God has no time for that, either. We should rather be looking first for the Kingdom of God and His righteousness. Because our Father knows our other needs and they will be met as they follow. For God is at the center, yet again.

Jesus gives us pictures of God's goodness in the fowls of the air and the lilies of the field, pointing out how much more the Father loves us than them. We are all the one unique creation of the same great God, who is this sermon's theme.

It is not for us to judge our fellows, for we shall all be judged in the same way by God, in due course. Meanwhile we shall know them by what they do. Words will not tell us that.

And finally, we are assured that He spoke with authority, because He and the Father are one. The Scribes and Pharisees could not do so; for they had no part in the Father.

Let us read this great sermon again and again, keeping at the very center of our thoughts the one great God whom Jesus came, not so much to tell us of, as to show us in Himself. Amen.
Selwyn

THINK ON THESE THINGS
Forgiveness takes so little time, but lasts for eternity.

PRAYER
God of gentleness and grace, who came to us before
we had repented and watches over us by day and night,
You receive the things we say and do each hour.
Let all we say and all we do bring glory to Your name.

Let us strive to love and serve our fellow men
as You loved and served each one of us. For You
bore our deepest grief and endured our worst pain.
Your love was tough enough for Calvary.
Dwell in us richly by Your Holy Spirit though we
thoughtlessly disregard Your healing and Your miracles

Forgive us that we have not trusted each other;
forgive us also that we have not trusted You.
The way to Life is narrow, but You
enrich it with Your joy. We bring our love
for we have nothing else to give,
and there is nothing else You want.

In the name of Father, Son and Holy Spirit,
God without end, Amen.

Peace, Be Still!

STILLING THE STORM

Anyone who has done healing work will know only too well how exhausting it is. For you are giving something of yourself, offering something profound and personal. And it was because He had cured the great multitude who came to Jesus that evening that the disciples got hold of a boat to take him to the other side for rest and relaxation. But a considerable storm blew up and being fishermen, they knew only too well how dangerous these storms can be and how quickly things can change.

So as a last resort, they turned to Him because we just might be able to do *something*. How exactly like us. He should turn to Him first in our times of trouble, for He will come to our aid and rescue us, even when all hope seems lost. But we have never stood next to God in a sinking boat, and neither had they. They had seen nothing, apart from His great skill as a healer, that would raise Him above any other man. They had not seem Him raise the dead, or feed the thousands, they had not heard his words of endless love for all mankind or seen His transfiguration. These were things yet to come.

But He saved them from an early grave; against all their hopes and expectations He saved them all. And slowly the hesitant wonder began to dawn, how could they explain authority like this, when even the sea and the winds obeyed Him! Not yet a revelation, of course, but surely the first astonishing doubt, perhaps the first straw in the wind that Simon Peter might almost have grasped, but could not quite hold onto.

And again, the echo of ourselves, this is precisely how we are, the hesitant wonder, the slowly dawning question of just who He might be and what He might do in our lives. Perhaps we have to know danger, feel fear, before we find how great is our God. And how wonderfully He deals with our problems

There is a disturbingly similar, though reversed situation, in the Garden of Gethsemane after the last supper. But here it is Jesus who is in mortal danger and the disciples who were asleep; they gave Him no comfort or assistance. He had awoken at once to their immediate danger in the boat, He had acted immediately to save them. But now they continued their sleep, for we are slow and lethargic in responding to His calls, though He is swift and compassionate in answering ours.

But perhaps this is the very first step we have to take when we begin to ask, "What manner of man is this?" Only later, when we have received Him into our hearts, can we answer with confidence and certainty, "Thou art the Christ, the Son of the living God."
Amen.
Selwyn

THINK ON THESE THINGS
The Prince of Peace calms our storms.

PRAYER

Lord of the wind and tempest who
on the sea of Galilee felt the power
of the storm and the raging waves,

We are your disciples who do not see
that we are safe with You, no matter
what perils we face in life.

You bring Your calmness to our lives and
we see what manner of man You are
when the winds and waves obey You.

The sea grew calm, for You created it and
the winds were still, for You are the God of peace.
And we are safe only when we are with You.
Amen.

Nicodemus

NICODEMUS

I like Nicodemus. I have a lot of time for him. In the first place he didn't wait for Jesus to find him, he took the initiative, he went to Jesus, and not out of idle curiosity, he really wanted to find the way to eternal life. and seemed to recognize that it was in Jesus he would find the way. And all this in the face of unwavering opposition, even hatred, from his own class, the Pharisees. No doubt that was why he came by night. But beyond that he was humble with a respect for Jesus that defied the views of his peers. He was a master of Israel, a ruler, yet he acknowledged straight away that Jesus was a Rabbi, and a man who came from God. Nevertheless he was confounded by our Lord's first answer, "Ye must be born again." But in context this is not surprising, for Jesus introduced him to the Holy Spirit on a scale Nicodemus had never been asked to contemplate before. Indeed, our Lord had not spoken of the Holy Spirit like this, even to His disciples, or anyone else, prior to this. It broke entirely new ground. Nor was he used to Christ's manner of speaking in metaphor, which John tells us, even the disciples found difficult to understand.

And there is no possible doubt that Jesus was speaking of the Holy Spirit, since a capital letter begins each such reference - as compared with lower case, in the same passages, when speaking of our own/other spirits. (v.6 is a good example).This very clear distinction is maintained throughout the account. It is not accident; it is a clear and deliberate distinction. Though not one that Nicodemus understood.

From the very first, Jesus made it clear that a man <u>must</u> be born of the Holy Spirit. Note the verb <u>must,</u> it is not and never was, an option. But the gap between Jesus' knowledge and Nicodemus' earthly understanding was too great. Well intentioned and respectful though Nicodemus was, he had no experience of the Holy Spirit and so could not understand what our Lord was saying to him. And there follow the sublime verses 15-21 which, sadly for Nicodemus, and good man though he was, he would not have understood either.

But we understand and it is we who <u>must</u> now take to heart our Lord's injunctions. So let us today welcome the Holy Spirit into our hearts, for without Him there is no salvation. And with Him and Christ there is life eternal. Selwyn

THINK ON THESE THINGS
You came by night to find the One light that would lead you to eternal life.

PRAYER
You came in darkness to the One light
who could show you the way to eternal life.
And it was only to you He spoke His words of truth
that offered you salvation in the Holy Spirit.

But you didn't see how much God loved you,
or that He gave you Jesus, His only son,
who spoke to you in the Spirit
when He said you must be born again.

For you hadn't heard of the Holy Spirit and didn't
understand the wonderful words of our Lord,
But when you heard, as you must have heard
of the wind blowing and the flames burning at Pentecost,

you would understand, at last, the new life
that awaited you when you were born again;
that you need not perish, but have everlasting
life, in Jesus Christ Your Redeemer.
Amen.

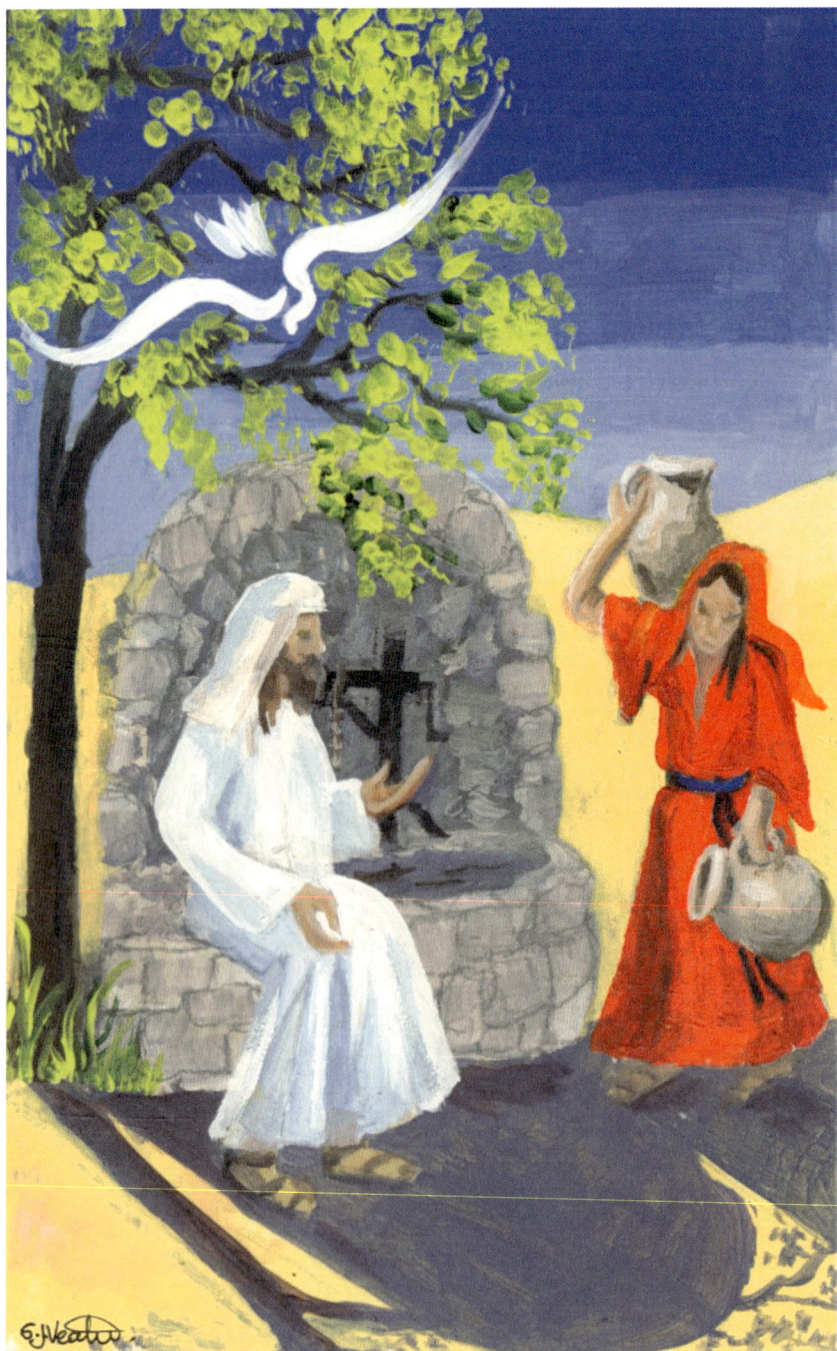

A Woman at the Well

AN ENCOUNTER WITH
A WOMAN AT THE WELL

Have you noticed how, when Jesus engaged with anyone, His conversation began with things that related to them, who they were or what was their interest, or way of life?

To the fishermen… "I will make you fishers of men."

To the lawyer… "Tell me what is written in the law!"

To the rich young ruler… "Go and sell your possessions and give to the poor!"

Today we meet a woman seeking water.

We find a thirsty, tired Jesus, sitting in the shade of Jacob's Well, resting while His disciples go shopping for food.

Along comes a Samaritan woman to collect water.

She came in the heat of the day to avoid meeting other women at the Well, they would come when it was cooler. She knew they despised her because of her life style, …she preferred to be alone. To her surprise she finds a Jewish man sitting there.

When He spoke to her, she was amazed… a Jew speaking to a Samaritan? And a woman too?

Her heart leapt when He offered her Living Water, which quenched all thirst permanently, …Oh what utter bliss, no more heavy water jars to carry, no more avoiding other women's disapproving stares and comments!

Of course, she had taken Him literally, just as Nicodemus had, "Can a man enter his mother's womb a second time?"

This woman, though immoral, was honest. "I have no husband!"

His total knowledge of her lifestyle astounded her!

"I've met a Prophet!" was her reaction. She spoke to Him of the coming Messiah.

"I am He," He says. Isn't it interesting that He told this Samaritan woman who He was, and yet waited for Peter's profession, "Thou art The Christ!" at Caesarea Philippi?

What does Jesus mean by Living Water? In St. John 7:37 He speaks of The Holy Spirit, that Holy Element essential for spiritual life, just as fresh water is essential for physical life.

So we learn that The Holy Spirit is that Living Water, essential for the worship of God, who is also Spirit.

Finally, let us return to the woman who set out to find water, what of her? She left her water jar behind, she, who avoided contact with others now rushes to tell all she meets that she has found the Messiah. Many, because of her witness became followers. Living Water flowed through her, because she had met Jesus at the well.

May that same Living Water flow through us!
Shirley

REFLECTION

Living water flowed through her, for she had met Jesus.

A WOMAN AT THE WELL

We thank you for the lessons You taught us
when You met a woman at the well,
for even when we do not know, or sense it,
God is speaking to us, offering us love.

Jesus you are the first to speak,
You come to us no matter what
our race or gender, for salvation
comes to us only from You.

We each have something we can give
the other, for we need our God each day
and where we worship does not matter, for
You delight to receive our earthly praise.

You tell us that the Father waits on them
who worship Him in spirit and in truth. And when
we tell each other of Your heavenly grace
then others follow, come with us as well.

So come to us as we stand and wait for water
from Your eternal truth. You give us to drink freely,
call us to Yourself and wait for us to come, in love
that speaks to us the tongues of men and angels. Amen.

PRAYER

You were so different, she essentially practical,
physical. Came to the well every day for water,
but left her waterpot so You could drink. She'd had
five husbands, maybe needed them as much as water.

We recognized authority, greater than ours
redeeming us to love and life eternal.
You willingly gave us everything,
Salvation was coming of the Jews.

You had a one-to-one conversation with her,
gave her precious time, so she knew that life
and time could be hers forever. We spend time
gloriously when we're with You.

And there's nothing more we need,
when we've been with the Son of God.
Amen.

GOOD SAMARITAN

Jesus, You are the Good Samaritan entering our lives when we are half dead to the things of the Spirit, binding our wounds, restoring us to the abundant life You came to give us.

You rescue us when we are overcome by life's assaults and bring us to a place of safety, for we are always safe with You, wherever You lead us.

And your final words were so caring... whatever it costs I will pay, for You say them without limit to Your love, without limit to Your pain.

You bring us to the heaven where we will suffer no more, but live in love and safety all the years of eternity... for there's no boundary to Your love.
Selwyn

THINK ON THESE THINGS
Whatever it costs, I will pay.

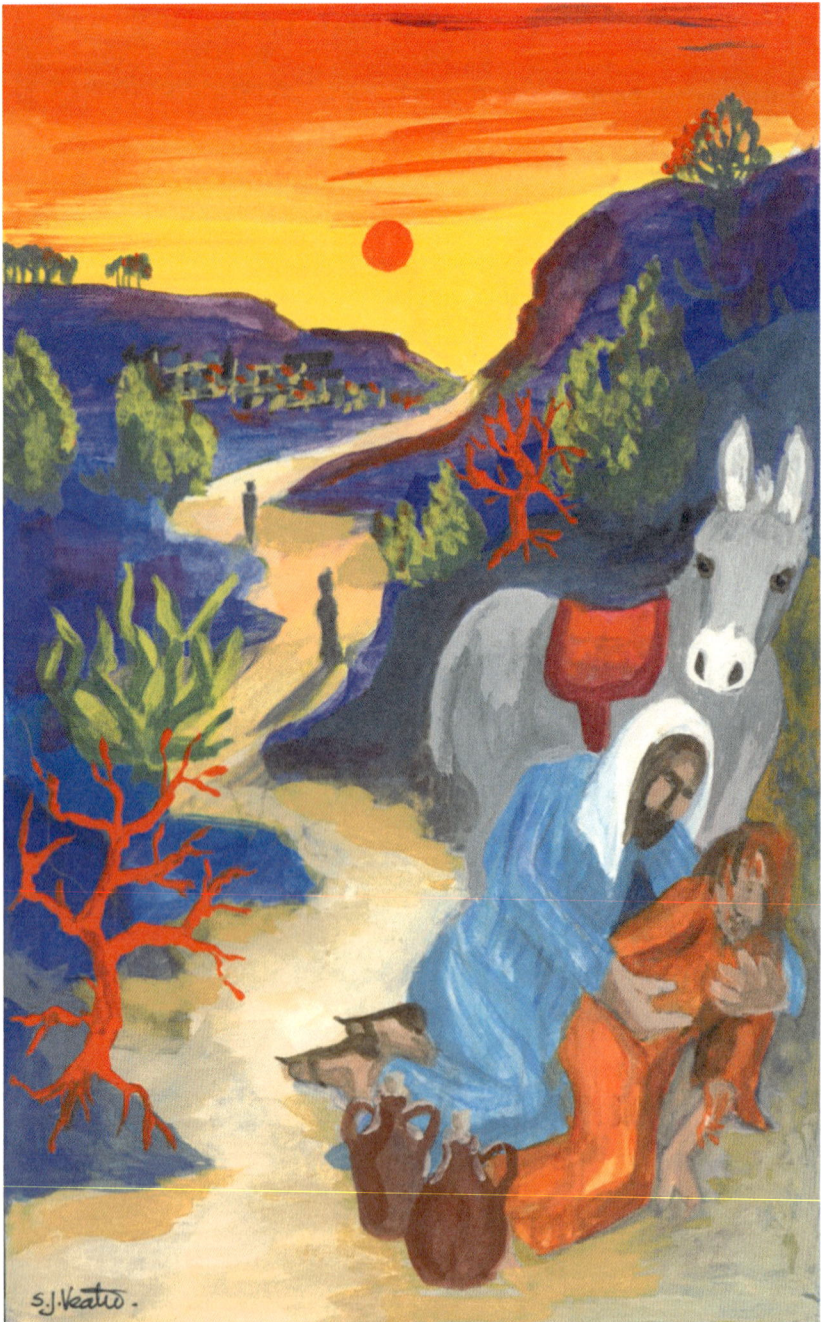

The Good Samaritan

PRAYER

Lord, we understand the final words
of the Good Samaritan
"Whatever it costs, I will pay,"
What wonderful words
to come from our Savior's lips,
words of unqualified love,
redeemed on Calvary.
Amen.

Welcome Home!

THE PRODIGAL SON

One who was lost is found.

When I was little I loved singing "Tell me the stories of Jesus" and this is one of my favorites.

A loving father has two sons. The younger one decides to go adventuring so he asks for his share of his inheritance. In other words he's wishing his father dead so he can get his hands on his money!

How that must have hurt the father, so ungrateful, so selfish, yet he agrees and shares the inheritance.

We hear of the riotous life this young man leads with false friends, prostitutes, just about anything went, and so did his money!

Then came famine.

No money, no friends, he found himself totally alone, hungry, the only job he could find was with pigs, the lowest of the low employment for a Jew. He had hit rock bottom.

The Holy Spirit hovered over him.

He began to come to his senses.

As he sat trying to pick bits to eat out of the pigs swill, he imagined the men employed by his father, working on his father's land, being well fed and honestly treated, paid a fair wage. What had he done?

If only he could go back! But how could he face his father after all the stupid things he'd done? After he'd hurt him so badly?

Inspired by the Holy Spirit, he begins to live in hope. Repentance is planted in his mind. He recognizes and admits his sin. He is willing to give up any privileges a son might have. Willing to be barefoot and work as a servant. He's prepared to beg for mercy.

He sets off, and as he travels he practices what he will say if his father will see him. At last his old home appears on the horizon. He feels nervous and ashamed as he remembers the harsh and hurtful words had uttered last time he was here.

As he approaches, whatever is this unusual sight he sees? A man running in his direction. How rare is that? No man ever ran in those days, it was undignified.

Then he recognized the runner, it was his father, arms outstretched in welcome, not at all what he expected! "Father I am no more worthy to be called your son"... He had uttered, but his father's arms were around him as they returned home together.

The father gives no lecture, no condemnation, just a warm welcome and more.

A robe is put on him giving him dignity and honor, a return to his family. A ring is put on his finger giving him authority and sonship. Sandals are put on his feet, he's a son, not a servant. Servants went barefoot.

What a happy homecoming! The family all together again... but NO. The elder son is resentful, hurt, jealous, all hateful emotions. He won't even acknowledge this boy as his brother, to his father he refers to him as "Your son". He refuses to go into the 'Welcome home' feast. In a way, HE now becomes the 'prodigal', going against his father's wishes.

Why did Jesus tell this story? To whom is He speaking? What message did He have for them? What lesson did He wish them to learn?

In Luke 15 we read that the tax collectors and sinners were gathered around Jesus, and within earshot were the Pharisees and teachers of the law, all complaining that, "This man welcomes sinners and even eats with them". So Jesus talks about Seeking the Lost, and heaven rejoicing over one sinner who repents.

He tells throughout the story how the Father, God, remains constant.

The younger son represents all who sin, dishonest tax collectors, thieves, liars, backbiters, adulterers, cheats, and us too.

The older son represents the Pharisees, Scribes, dishonest lawyers, the self-righteous, those who speak with their lips the right words, but don't believe in their hearts. God the Father watches every day, and patiently waits. The Holy Spirit plants in the sinful, that desire to repent so that estrangement may dissolve into harmony and love.

How does this apply to us?

We learn that our free will allows us to wander away from God. It shows us that life lived afar off from God is never good for very long.

It guides us into realization that we need, with the help of the Holy Spirit, to be sincerely sorry and to seek true repentance.

It advises us that we should welcome sinners with absolutely no judgment.

The parable beautifully demonstrates to us God's Grace. And if we truly repent, teaches us that God will forgive us and welcome us home.

Shirley

THINK ON THESE THINGS
Your Father's servants have bread enough and to spare.

PRAYER
Lord, forgive us when we want everything,
and when we want it now. Forgive us
when we waste our gifts on things
that are unworthy of Your grace.

We demean the image You made in us
with things that please us for a time but wither
in a day and are no more. For by Your grace and
in Your care we see how shallow are our ways,

We are too flawed to glorify Your anointed Son who
takes away the daily sins we live and turns our steps

toward our home again and to a loving God who waits
and watches every day, greets us with open arms.

We are inadequate to bring Your love to a skeptical
society.
So show them the mercy of Your ways, and bring them
to see your goodness and your grace, how great Thou art,
redeeming all mankind in Jesus, Your precious son,
Amen.

Peter at Caesarea Philippi

CAESAREA PHILIPPI

This is a remarkable chapter and Matthew 16 gives us a full account of the incident. It is a chapter about Christ's identity.

Our Lord's question did not come out of the blue. It arose directly from a dispute with the Pharisees and Sadducees, challenging Christ to prove his identity by a sign from heaven. Which He refused, not from churlishness, *He* was never that way, but because He knew they would not understand signs from heaven, if He did.

The issue was fundamental. They were talking to the son of God and it is difficult to see what greater sign they could have expected. If they could not see God when they were talking to Him, what sign would convince them? They parted, refusing or unwilling to recognize His identity. So subsequently He warned His disciples to beware the leaven of the Pharisees.

The highest level of religious authority had rejected Him. So when they arrived at Caesarea Philippi, He naturally wanted to find out what ordinary people thought of Him. And He was not much more successful in that.

Admittedly they respected Him more than their leaders had done, but they attributed to Him all sorts of identities, some Elisha, some John the Baptist etc. But no-one in the whole of His community saw His real identity as the Christ. So, He asked His disciples, "But who do *you* say that I am?"

And to his everlasting praise it was Simon Peter who confessed, "Thou art the Christ, the Son of the living God." What a momentous reply. A single voice against the world. No wonder that Jesus replied that flesh and blood had not told him this. There can be little doubt that it was the Holy Spirit who had revealed it to him. And perhaps it was at that moment that Christ decided that Peter was the man to lead His Great Commission and feed His sheep.

At all events He extolled Peter for his perception. Not something for which Peter was often commended, so much as his courage and rock-like steadfastness.

Peter's was the first small seed of our Lord's mission. A single voice, but a wonderful one. And one from which people and nations have drawn their faith for centuries. Marvelous things happen when we recognize our Lord and hail Him as the Christ.

Selwyn

THINK ON THESE THINGS
You are the Christ; the Son of the living God.

PRAYER
Dear Lord Jesus, help us to praise You when
others do not see Your grace. We struggle
against spirits of malice toward Your high example.
So may Your holy life illuminate our way

in righteous light, that we may glorify
Your name with joy before all we meet.
Confront us with Your eternal sacrifice that we
may reverence Your work and so lift others to
eternal life with God the Father, Son and Holy Spirit.
Let us glorify You where You live in grace and peace,
and may the words we speak extol the Kingdom
where we shall live with You in Your eternal rest.
Amen.

The Transfiguration

THE TRANSFIGURATION
EYEWITNESSES OF HIS MAJESTY

"While he was still speaking, suddenly a bright cloud overshadowed them..." (Matthew 17:5).

"Jesus, however, shines from within; he does not simply receive light but he is himself light from light."
Pope Benedict XV1

The Holy Trinity is present at the Transfiguration of Jesus. The exact words uttered by the Father at the Baptism of Jesus were repeated at the Transfiguration. The Father spoke from a shining cloud, the Holy Spirit, saying: "This is my Son, the Beloved; with him I am well pleased...." (Matthew 17:5). This voice of the Father revealing his Son issued forth from a bright shining cloud. Clouds were often in Holy Scripture combined with light, a symbol of the Holy Spirit. The Father spoke by and through an overshadowing cloud of light. As we will see, the Holy Spirit was also very involved in the events leading up to the Transfiguration.

As the revealer of Glory, the Holy Spirit was present to disclose to Peter who Jesus was. In Luke's Gospel, Jesus was praying alone, although near the disciples (Luke 9:18-20). "Who do the crowds say that I am?" asked Jesus. "But who do you say that I am?" he asked the disciples. Peter answered, "You are the Messiah, the Son of the living God" (Matthew 16:16). Jesus proceeded to inform these disciples that "flesh and blood has not revealed this to you" (Matthew 16:17). The Holy Spirit, the revealer of Glory through the Father, had revealed to Peter who Jesus was. The Transfiguration likely could not have been exposed before this revelation to Peter. Later, in Gethsemane, these same three men were to keep watch in the garden during the agony of Jesus. They were eyewitnesses to the brightest light of the Holy Spirit and the most profound darkness ever to take place on Earth. Jesus, knowing that his crucifixion was soon to occur, gave these three men the glorious light in the shining cloud to increase their faith in who he indeed was. Jesus was the light of light, the true God of true God. And Jesus was being revealed directly to the dazzled disciples.

This light shown at the Transfiguration was not a light as the light that showed "on" the face of Moses as he was given a direct word from God. Therefore, the light of Jesus was no outside light. Instead, this light was an inner light shining out of the very being of his Father. This was a radiant splendorous light, a light whiter than white. Later, Peter looked back to this event in his second epistle. One can feel the rapturous memory of the Transfiguration as Peter scrambles to describe this Earth-shattering event. Peter describes the events with ecstasy to increase the faith of the believers listening. "We were eyewitnesses of his majesty," he exclaims (2 Peter1:16). Peter tells his listeners, "You will do well to be attentive to this as to a lamp shining in a dark place, until the day dawns and the morning star rises in your hearts" (2 Peter 1:19). And his final admonition was to make sure that the hearers knew scripture is not, nor ever will be a matter of human interpretation unless they are moved from the Holy Spirit spoke from God. Peter realized that the Holy Spirit revealed to him that Jesus was the Messiah. Peter knew that the shining cloud revealed the Glory of God on the Holy Mountain. And it was Peter at Pentecost who spoke as a man of great wisdom, which he was not, that Jesus had received from the Father the promise of the Holy Spirit. He declared that the Holy Spirit was poured out so that people could see and hear (Acts1: 33). It is worth mentioning that this same Holy Spirit today needs people sensitive to the pouring out of his mighty power. As was with Jesus, this seeing and hearing come only through communication in prayer, devotion, and communion. May our faith be increased, as it was in the disciples, by hearing God's voice often by the presence of the shining cloud. Amen.

Martha

PRAYER
Dear Lord Jesus,
Simon Peter knew by the Spirit that You were the Son of God when You took three disciples to a mountain top. And You were praying with the Father when You were transfigured and they saw, beyond the flesh, Your divine, celestial glory.

Perhaps we're all a little transfigured when we pray.

You alone were clothed in shining white,
above the prophets, above us all.
And from above, Your Father's voice
spoke out Your role, our Savior and our King.

Peter wanted to stay and build three tabernacles,
to escape from the world for a while. But soon
you were back down the mountain, again.
The world doesn't leave you alone for long.

But we shall never forget that moment's majesty
or how great Thou art, even when You were humblest,
when You were one of us.
Amen.

TRANSFIGURATION
ST. JOHN REMEMBERS

"I will never forget that day! Jesus took my brother James, Peter, and me up the mountain to pray. He often went off to pray, so this was nothing new for us, but this day was different.

We prayed and when we looked at Jesus, it was as though His face was shining like the sun, and His clothes were so bright white, it hurt my eyes to look at Him!

Stranger still, there beside Him was Moses, not shining like Jesus, but I remember reading in Scripture how Moses's face glowed after receiving God's Commandments.

Elijah was there too, the greatest of ancient prophets, speaking with Jesus.

We watched in awe and amazement as the three conversed together!

Then I remember a shining cloud came, it covered them, and this voice came from the Cloud, "This is My beloved Son, listen to Him!"

That was awesome, we fell on our faces, we couldn't look any more, we lay prostrate, we knew this was something incredibly special. What an honor to hear the Voice of God, in the presence of the Word of God and The Light of the World. How honored we felt and awe-struck! What would happen next?

Then Jesus came and stood by us. "Come on," He said, "We must go back to the others."

Peter had a brilliant idea, "Let's build three Tabernacles right here on the mountain, One for You Jesus, One for Moses and One for Elijah, then we can stay here and worship!"

"Oh no," said Jesus, "There is work to be done, we must return. Remember to tell no-one about what you have seen until after the resurrection."

I wondered at the time what He meant by "After The Resurrection."

The memory of those dark days that were soon to follow, hang heavy in my heart to this day.

Judas leaving our last meal together, then the arrest in Gethsemane. Oh, how ashamed I feel that Peter, James, and I fell asleep when He needed us to keep watch.

We felt lost and very afraid after His crucifixion. It felt like the end had come… but then I remembered that shining face glowing on the mountain top! I remembered His words. "Tell no-one until after The Resurrection." So really the Transfiguration was the fore-runner to the glorious New Life in Christ."

Let us too spread the glorious news of The Resurrection of Jesus, and that The Love of God encompasses us all.

Shirley

REFLECTION
Perhaps we are all a little transfigured when we pray.

PRAYER
Two essential things were required of the
three disciples, as they are required of us all
before we may see the transfigured Christ.

They, and we, must be quite apart from the world,
as the scriptures say they were, and we must be
very close to Jesus for only three were chosen.

And the wonderful experience would be beyond forgetting,
would be implanted in their hearts and minds forever,
For the curtain of flesh was parted; And they saw Jesus as
He truly is.

For He alone was in perfect white, above both Moses
and Elias, above all prophets, above all men, for You alone
are the Holy one of God.

Father, we thank You that on the mountain, Jesus was
twice confirmed as the son of God. If the miracles and
the teaching and the presence were not enough,

they saw the evidence with their own eyes, and also
heard the voice from the shining cloud proclaiming
He was God's son. They cannot have mistaken both.

It strengthened our Lord for His crucifixion and strengthened His disciples, too. Lord Jesus, is there nothing You would not do to make us Yours?

We saw God and Jesus as one, and both were light, Light from light, Light from His face and light from the cloud, showing us the truth, that He was there for us.

But soon they had to return to life
that awaited them down the mountain,
The world does not leave us alone for long.
Amen.

LAZARUS

It's not surprising that Lazarus was sick; or that Martha and Mary asked Jesus to come and heal him.

Jesus *always* comes to us when we are sick or in trouble. Nor even that Jesus, knowing the Jews wanted to stone Him to death, nevertheless still came. It is so typical of our Lord to ignore the worst of dangers, completely, when we call Him and our wellbeing is at stake. However, He waited awhile before He went to Bethany, for He knew that Lazarus was dead and He wanted His visit to be stunning enough for the disciples to believe, The principal reason for His delay was the faith of His disciples

Martha went out to meet Him and said at once that if He had been there, Lazarus would not have died. Our Lord reassured her with wonderful words, "I am the resurrection and the life. He that believeth on me, though he were dead, yet shall he live," Martha then went to fetch Mary, who repeated Martha's words that had Jesus been here her brother would not have died. For when we are with Jesus, we are always safe, and we shall never die.

Jesus wept and groaned within Himself, then commanded them to take away the stone. But Mary said he had been dead four days and 'stinketh' to which our Lord replied with the fundamental principle of His mission, that faith enables everything, "Did I not tell you, Mary, that when you believe you will see the glory of God." For He knew that time and death were at His command. Then He

' Lazarus, Come Forth ! '

prayed aloud, saying "Lazarus come forth," and the dead man came out of his tomb. Jesus commanded that he should be unbound and let go.

For Lazarus' rising had proved that, in Jesus, there is rich life after death in His name, His power over the grasp of death and time had been conclusively displayed, His love for human kind established beyond question. So much so that some of the Jews believed, though some reported back to the Pharisees who from that day onwards, plotted to put Him to death. They issued an edict that anyone who knew His whereabouts must report it, (so they could take and kill Him). But Jesus went with His disciples to Ephraim.

And soon after this, he dined again at Bethany and Lazarus dined with them. Oh, to have heard a little of what they said to each other, or to see the life in Lazarus' face, and how happy our Lord was, spending time with His human friends where He loves and is loved.

I may be quite wrong, of course, but I cannot avoid the sense that in His sublime words we sense the closeness of eternity, and nothing that disturbs an everlasting peace, a peace that passes our understanding.

Amen.

Selwyn

THINK ON THESE THINGS
I am the Resurrection and the Life.
When you believe you will see the glory of God.

PRAYER

Lord You came to Bethany, defied the danger
of Your own death for your friends, as You
always hazard death for us. For You control
and temper the harshness of time and death.

And when You wept for Lazarus, You wept for
all our deaths. Martha came to You in her trouble
as we all come to You in our troubles and in our distress
You promise us that we shall see the glory of God.

Mary came to his tomb, weeping, and on the
other side of her tears, saw how You have power
to conquer death; and we understand that
though we may die, yet in You we shall live.

As You raised Lazarus and set him free,
so free us from our evil natures and lift us
to unending love, in the name of the God
who gave us His unending love, in You.
Amen.

LAZARUS IS RAISED

Dear Lord, You came to bitterness and grief
where You had always been a welcome guest.
for Lazarus was four days dead.
And when You wept for Lazarus
You wept for all our deaths.

So You taught Martha that when we believe
we shall see the glory of God. And she saw,
on the other side of her tears, how God
has power to conquer death.

So Lazarus rose and we understood Your words, that You
are the resurrection and the life, and that even though we
die, yet shall we live in You.
Even so Lord, we shall never forget that
You are the eternal life and in You there is no death at all.
Amen.

THINK ON THESE THINGS
Those You love know they cannot live without You.

PRAYER
Lamb of God, who takes away the sins
of the world, bring me to those who
have nothing and let me give them of myself.

You came to Bethany to raise Your friend,
Lazarus, though he was four days dead, for
only You can temper the harshness of death,

and when You wept for Lazarus, You wept
for all our deaths. Martha came to You
in her troubles, as we all come to You

in our troubles, and You comforted her,
saying that when we believe we shall see
the glory of God for You are His glory and His love.

Mary came to his tomb in human grief,
but saw on the other side of her tears
how God has power to conquer death,

and we understood Your words, Lord,
that though we be dead, yet shall we live.
So raise us to eternal life with You,

for You are the Resurrection and the Life.
Amen.

THE LAST SUPPER

Jesus asked James and me to go and prepare a place to share the Passover meal with Him and the other Apostles. He told us to look out for a man carrying a water pitcher! Now that's an unusual thing to try and find. Collecting water is women's work!

Well I never! Just look, there is a man indeed doing just that!

As instructed we followed him to a house, and there told the man in charge that, "The Master has sent us." Sure enough he led us to an upper room. It was all set up in readiness. So we completed the preparations, and returned to find Jesus and the others.

That evening at dusk, we gathered there, all thirteen of us. I thought the Master seemed more thoughtful and quieter than usual, there was a sort of sadness to Him, as though He thought this may be the last time we would share a meal together?

What did He know that we didn't?

Suddenly He stood up, and holding the unleavened bread in His hands, He gave thanks and blessed it, "This is my body" He said, "Broken for you," and He broke the bread into pieces and gave it to us in turn. Whatever did He mean?

'This is My Body'

I remember seeing Him break five small barley loaves into pieces, and with that tiny amount, five thousand hungry people were fed. Has He a way of feeding even more people with this bread? His Body?

As supper continued, we asked each other, "What do you think He means?"

Then He quite upset us. He dipped a sop into the dish and said, "One of you will betray me!" I just couldn't believe my ears! All of us gave up our trades and professions to follow Him, and be with Him, whoever would even think of betraying Him?, and to whom? We all asked, "Is it I, Lord?" I wondered if I had done something to let Him down.

Judas Iscariot could bear it no more; he got up to leave. The Master said "What you are about to do, do quickly."

Oh, it must be an errand the Master has asked him to run, after all, he is the purse keeper. I wonder what it is!

When we had finished the food, Jesus lifted up His cup of wine, gave thanks and said, "This is my blood of the New Covenant, shed for you, and for many for the remission of sins, drink this, and remember me."

Jesus then left the table; He picked up a towel and tied it around His waist.

The water bowl for foot washing was, as usual, by the door. He poured water into the bowl and started to wash our feet, as though He was our servant!

When it got to Peter's turn, can you imagine! Impetuous Peter tried to stop Him, but when the Master said "Unless I wash your feet, you have no part in me!" Then, of course Peter threatened to strip down, and have Jesus wash him all over! Typical Peter!, never a dull moment!

I realize now, He was giving us an example that as followers of Him, we must serve others, sometimes doing the lowliest of jobs, like kneeling and washing even a beggar's feet.

When the task was finished, we sang a hymn, and then He led us out into the bright moonlit night. We strolled into the Garden of Gethsemane on the Mount of Olives.

"Stay here a while, I will go a little further on to pray. You three, watch and pray for me."

He went about thirty odd yards ahead of us, He knelt, buried His head in His hands… "Father if it is possible, let this cup pass from me, but not my will but…" silence.

I and the other apostles had fallen asleep.

Shirley

THINK ON THESE THINGS
You knew Judas would betray You, and You were willing to wash his feet.

PRAYER

Lord Jesus, because our God is pure
You took water and washed our feet, that,
being washed by You we might be clean
and share your sanctity and grace.

For though we do not understand the love
with which God washes our feet, we know
You free us from our stains, so we never
strive again for earthly consequence.

We take Your little meals of bread and wine
made sacred by Your presence with us,
feast on the truth that redeems us all
and the love that brings salvation.

And though You eat with one who will betray You,
You go Your way to the dark garden, pray, then
call him friend when he betrays You with a kiss.
Forgiveness had no end for You, either.
Amen.

Holy Communion

HOLY COMMUNION
HOLY SPIRIT AND SACRAMENTAL MYSTERY

"The cup of blessing that we bless, is it not a sharing in the blood of Christ? The bread that we break, is it not a sharing in the body of Christ?" (1 Corinthians 10:16)

"Our embarrassment of riches is perhaps most obvious as we seek greater understanding of divine mysteries, such as the work of the Holy Spirit in the liturgy, and particularly of His work in the Eucharist." Dr. Michael Gama

Wherever the Holy Spirit is mentioned in Holy Scriptures, there appears to be a sense of unbelievable mystery, power, revelation, and creation. As the third Person of the Holy Trinity, the Holy Spirit seems to be involved in every aspect of the Father's and Son's mission for redemption and salvation of humanity. Wherever the unexpected occurs, the implausible transpires, and the impossible ensues, the Holy Spirit appears. Is it not true, although hidden, that in the Holy Eucharist, the Person of the Holy Spirit shows up mysteriously? Liturgical Churches have a word for this appearance called 'epiclesis,' an invocation of the Holy Spirit upon the bread and wine during the Eucharistic Prayer. The priest at this place in the liturgy asks God to send the Holy Spirit to perform and transform ordinary elements of Earth into supernatural, mystical, and life-giving spiritual power. As John Paul 11 states, at this moment "comes strength to live the Christian life and zeal to share that life with others." We see the Holy Spirit once more, as the wind from nowhere outwardly seen, perform a powerfully transformative and supernatural act of conversion.

We observe the Holy Spirit poised above the waters at creation, bringing chaos to order in a freshly created world. The Holy Spirit also brings chaos to order through the miraculous dynamism in His role in the Holy Eucharist. We cannot see Him with our physical eyes, but as St. Thomas Aquinas aptly states: "But a dauntless faith believes." As Christians, we believe in the invisible and fearless power of a Person, the Third Person of the Holy Trinity, to completely transform us into the likeness of Jesus Christ.

How completely exhilarating when one truly grasps the beautiful and magnificent Person of the Holy Spirit. So many of us are bored and tired of ordinary life as we know it. The Spirit can turn our ordinary bread and wine into life-giving energy, transformational influence, and genuine fullness of life! We witness the unseen Spirit doing only what he can do right before our eyes. Magic has no part of this process. We are not deceived. It is genuine because we experience this miraculous vitality engulfing every aspect of our lives. Love becomes possible, even for our enemies. Joy becomes manifested even in the minutest aspects of life. Health becomes an asset even when our bodies are ridden with disease. The Holy Spirit brings Heaven to Earth, and as Joseph discovered in the Old Testament, things meant to harm us can be turned for our good.

One could ask: "What is the purpose of the Holy Eucharist, aside from the personal transformation of participants into saints?" That purpose alone would be unbelievable. However, as seen at Pentecost, the Holy Trinity adores relational community, especially the Holy Spirit. With all the differences represented at any time in the Holy Eucharist, unity is present within a community of believers. The Holy Spirit is miraculously able to bring people together in love and peace. He, the Spirit, is a unifier. This unification is not only with other people but also within the individual. Without the presence of the Spirit living within us, how torn and disrupted we live our little lives. Today we want this, and tomorrow that. Today we are sad, and tomorrow we are happy and contented. The Holy Spirit, through participation with other believers, we gradually but unquestionably come to want only one thing, Jesus Christ living in us, sustained by the guidance and support of the Holy Spirit.

It is helpful to become familiar with the miraculous power of the Holy Spirit in the Holy Eucharist. He is quiet and unassuming, never pushing Himself on us. To seek Him and be aware of His working in all of our lives is a worthy endeavor, especially His work in the Holy Eucharist.

Martha

REFLECTION

You gave us Holy Communion. You wanted us to be together, always.

PRAYER

You longed to share the Passover with Your disciples
and we, too, may share Your bread and wine
when we come to Your table as disciples.

You chose an ordinary room, but You sanctify
the places where we meet, and we are your people
who long to share Communion with You..

So invite us to Your table, bring us to the elements
where Your body is broken and Your blood is shed
that we may share in Your new covenant of love.

And though our hearts are heavy when \you suffer,
we remember that You loved us to the end, for You
are life and eternal truth. And You never change.

So we do these things in remembrance of You.
Amen.

GETHSEMANE
THE BOTTOM OF EVERYTHING

"I am deeply grieved, even to death; remain here and stay with me."

Gethsemane is an estate garden at the bottom of the Mount of Olives. The word Gethsemane means Oil Press. Jesus was at the lowest point in his human and earthly life on the evening before his arrest and the day before his Crucifixion. Here he was crushed. We have all found ourselves at such a point after having long periods of joy, success, and exhilaration. Suddenly, we find ourselves at the bottom of the emotional mountain, desolate and alone. He had taken the same three disciples into the Garden with him who accompanied him on the Mount of Transfiguration, Peter, James, and John. "I am deeply grieved, even unto death; remain here, and stay awake with me." At the point of His most significant need, His companions abandoned Him. Jesus had given his entire being for their welfare and edification for three years. They needed Jesus because the Holy Spirit had not yet been sent to them as a comforter. Now Jesus needed them. They fell asleep. However, the more painful truth was they had no genuine empathy nor deep concern for His grief.

Jesus' demeanor became utterly other than what we see anywhere else in Holy Scripture. Yet, just moments before, He was walking along as always. But then, it was as if the reality of the bottom of life hit Him in a gut-wrenching debilitating manner. The veneer of life was ripped away.

The Garden of Gethsemane

We all know those moments when the unexpected changes us forever; the death of a child, the loss of a spouse, the abandonment of a friend. We see. But the vision is hopelessness. It feels as if nothing remains of us. Lost cannot adequately describe our state. We must now face the real ordeal. The actual Cross lies ahead. The authentic Cross cannot be anywhere as devastating as Gethsemane. The Cross will be after we can no longer experience pain. In Gethsemane, pain is raw, heightened, and inconsolable. All that remains in Gethsemane is the rubble of a life in tatters and incapable of ever being put back together in the same way as before. All that remains is the presence of the Holy Spirit!

Jesus wavers in His humanity back and forth between His human will and the Father's will. Then, in a split cosmic second, He falls to the ground in significant drops of sweat filled with blood. Eventually, come the words we all must say: "My Father, if this cannot pass unless I drink it, your will be done." The Holy Trinity was fully present. Resignation supervened. The Holy Spirit, the comforter, friend, supporter, and breath of life, strengthened Him and gave Him all Jesus needed to silently surrender to becoming the sacrificial Lamb who would take away the Sin of the whole world.

It was in a Garden where mankind lost its innocence. And it would be in a Garden of despair where humanity regained its dignity as it transformed from lost to found. The irony happens in our own lives, too. The things that Satan intends to be vessels of destruction through the power of the Holy Spirit become instruments and means whereby our greatest good evolves. In this life, we will never be free from those times of sheer shock and anguish. New life will restore what was lost through the sustaining and "remaining" Person of the Holy Spirit. From the loss will come the catalyst for a purpose greater than ourselves. Through our own Gethsemane, the Holy Spirit will convert us into powerful witnesses to how overcoming power is possible for all who believe. Through the Spirit, the vision of reality without a purpose will become a cornerstone of hope for a world lost in its gardens of agony (Matthew 26). Martha

THINK ON THESE THINGS
You know the pain it will cost to be the Savior of the world.

A PRAYER FOR YOU, LORD, AT GATHSEMANE
Grant me to feel as close to You now as I did
in the human hours of Gethsemane. Help me
to pray for You in the darkness of a silent garden
that this undeserved cup might pass from You.

But only You could drink it, because I
would not turn from my wicked ways.
How much I longed to ease Your sorrow,
yet could not watch with You one hour.

Did Satan remind You about those You'd healed,
but deserted You now, ask why You should die
for people like that, for people like me? Did
even You wonder in the long hours of the night?

Here there is only anguish and danger,
and though I want so much to protect You,
they will come and take You away
to mockery, and derision, and death.

Now I know how much You will suffer for me
when they crucify You for what I have done.
Only when it's over and I am bitter in my regret
will I understand why I love You so much.
Amen.

At the foot of the Cross

CRUCIFICTION (1)
A CENTURION RECALLS THE
FIRST GOOD FRIDAY

Oh how I long to return to Rome with her fragrant pine trees and beautiful fountains! I've had enough of these Jews with all their petty squabbles, the narrow streets, the heat, and the flies. Last week there were hundreds of Jews waving palm branches over at the Eastern gate. A man riding on a donkey rode in. They believe that that's the gate their Savior from the Romans will come in by, but surely not riding on a donkey! It all went off peacefully, but we have to keep a watch on these things. It was all harmless enough.

I'm on duty today. Three to be crucified. I hate this, so barbaric. You should hear the screams when the nails are driven in, and always a crowd comes to watch, it makes me sick to the core.

The culprits are stripped naked, serve them right, they shouldn't go thieving and killing. My men divide the clothes between them. Anything decent they cast lots for. It disgusts me.

We arrived at Golgotha. Just look at the scene. The one in the middle has been beaten and scourged. He's covered in blood. He's bruised and still bleeding. They've mocked Him and He has a wreath of twisted thorns plaited into a rough crown rammed on to His head. Beads of blood like berries have formed on it. He remains quiet and there's a sort of dignity about Him. The other two are shouting out and swearing. One yells at Him to save Himself, and them! Who is this one then? There's a notice written above His head, let's look, *The King of the Jews.* Surely not the man who's done miraculous things? My colleague told me how this man healed his servant without having to visit, he was always talking about how his having faith had made the miracle happen.

Oh look, there's a little group standing silently near the cross. Three women and a man. I reckon that's His Mother and three friends come to support her.

How calm she is. She must be in shock. What an ordeal.

Listen, He is speaking.

"Father forgive, they know not what they do."

What a saint to ask forgiveness for His tormentors and people who are killing Him. That's very unusual. The normal cries from crosses are full of hate and expletives. This man is unique!

Now He's just promised the thief next to Him he will be in Paradise just because he has confessed his sin and said sorry. He sounds more like a god than a man!

Ah! I was right, that lady is His Mother. He's just put her into the care of His friend. She must be a widow with no one to care for her now He is being killed.

How cold it's turning and how dark. It's more like night than day. This really is odd. I feel apprehensive, this isn't normal. The crowd has gone quiet too.

He's calling out again. "My God, why have you forsaken me?"

We realize that this is the moment that Jesus takes the weight of all the sin of the world into Himself. That sin has cut Him off from God, because no sin can come into the presence of God." He descended into hell".

The Holy Spirit upheld Him throughout His ordeal.

Now that source of Living Water says He is thirsty.

"Give Him some vinegar and hyssop, that will cure His thirst, hurry up there."

"It is finished," says Jesus. Silence falls again.

"Father, into Your hands I commend my spirit."

He's talking to His Father again, that was the first word He spoke, 'Father'

He must be close to Him whoever He is.

Its three pm, an order has come through to break the criminals legs, to hurry the deaths before the Sabbath. See to it men, hurry up."

To their surprise they find that Jesus is already dead.

What they don't realize is that Jesus was not killed by

them, but He gave His life voluntarily. He made the supreme sacrifice, sustained by the Holy Spirit.

"Surely this man was The Son of God."

Thunder rumbled, lightning flashed, Jesus was dead. But the Holy Spirit remained.

The Holy Spirit was very much alive.
Shirley

REFLECTION
You show Your divinity in every torment you forgive.

PRAYER
Dear Lord Jesus,
Today there is nothing I can ask of You,
no need of mine is worthy to compare
with Your eternal sacrifice for me.
Today You will give me everything
though I am not worthy of Your love.

And You will stamp the world forever
with the image of Your cross.
You will be without honor or respect
but You will earn, forever, the name of God.
Soon I will come to You again
with my pain and my prayers
for the sick and those I love.

But today there is nothing I can ask.

Today, I can think only of You, Amen.

THERE WAS NO MUSIC WHEN YOU DIED
Dear Lord,
There was no music when You died,
we grieved in silence, We could not sing
until You rose again, for You are the meaning
in our songs.
And the love of Christ is in our minds.

You come to us in risen majesty
and we praise You with our voices
salute You with rhythm, for You
have given us resurrection life.

We cannot worship You as angels do,
but grant, O Lord, that we may sing
our anthems for love of You
whose music fills our hearts.

And in our singing, Jesus,
may Your name be ever blessed
and in Your mercy
hear our songs.
Amen.

The Nails

CRUCIFIXION (2)
THE NAILS

The nails they used to pin our Lord to His cross had to bear the full weight of the dying Christ. So they were big and barbarous and undoubtedly added materially to His pain.

They seemed to pin Him into isolation. He would suffer and die alone on His cross. But in reality He would never be closer, because He was suffering and dying for *us*. And those who jeered and mocked Him did so only because they did not understand that He was doing it for them; doing it for all mankind.

And even when it was all over, they would still have made it difficult to take His body down without further tearing His flesh. It seems there was nothing good that could be said of them.

And yet, despite all that, they are wonderful instruments of grace to me and I view them with a gratitude that is almost holy. Because they were also the first and clearest evidence of His resurrection. When He appeared to His disciples in the Upper Room for the first time after His Resurrection, it was the marks of the nails that showed His disciples that it was indeed their crucified Lord. And there was good reason for His doing so. Because they were cold, inanimate objects who could not lie and who had no reason to deceive us. They showed that He had died and now was risen again for He was standing before them. Their imprints provided indisputable evidence for His Resurrection. They could not be ignored or argued away.

I know of no other credible interpretation of their marks. Their evidence came in two separate forms. They could be seen and they *were* seen; they could be touched and our Lord invited His disciples to do just that. Their evidence was close to being indisputable. In the end, they persuaded even doubting Thomas that he was in the presence of his Lord and his God.

So I give thanks this day for the terrible and wonderful evidence of the resurrection in the marks of the nails. Without them the disciples might not have believed and we would never have come closer to our great and immortal God.

It is one more thing He suffered for us. And one more reason to worship our beloved and amazing God in Jesus Christ, our Lord. Amen.

Selwyn

THINK ON THESE THINGS
Nails and death could not compare with the power of the Holy Spirit.

PRAYER
We thank you Lord that you did not leave us
without evidence we could both see and touch,
to show us You had risen from the dead.

We feel Your suffering the more and worship You

the stronger for seeing the hideous marks of the nails
in Your hands and feet, the spear marks in Your side.

Let us involve Your love in every situation we encounter,
proclaim the God who lives and died for us, who paid
the one eternal ransom for all who believe on His name.

So, design us for greater service in Your kingdom,
let us throng about Your empty tomb and flaunt to all
our joy in our everlasting Savior and our God,
in the name of the Resurrected Jesus, Amen.

'Woman, why do you weep?'

RESURRECTION (1)
MARY MAGDALENE REMEMBERS

I love Jesus. He found me when I was lost. I was a dreadful sinner, possessed by demons, living a wretched life style. I felt degraded and unhappy, trapped with no hope of a way out.

Then I met Jesus, and He healed me.

It was so wonderful! My life was completely turned around. I followed Him and did all that I could to help Him. I heard Him preach, saw Him heal others, it was amazing! He was so gentle, yet had such an authority about Him. When He spoke you felt you just had to listen! How did it all end up like that?

Last Friday was the worst day of my life.

There's all sorts of stories going around. They say that Judas, one of His disciples, a close follower actually sold Him for thirty pieces of silver, the price of a slave! Can you believe it? But then Judas was always more interested in money than people. He was the one who criticized me for "wasting" my precious Spikenard on Jesus's feet! He said it should have been sold to help the poor. Sold to help Judas himself is more like!

When I stood with the other Mary, Jesus's Mother, her sister also called Mary, at the foot of the Cross, my heart was breaking. I tried so hard to be strong. Mary, His mother was so composed, and Jesus, even with all He was going through had concern for her future, and asked John to take care of her now she was a widow with no son to look after her as she got older.

We laid Him in Joseph of Arimathea's new tomb, when we took Him down from the Cross. The day was nearly over, we didn't have time to use our herbs and oils to prepare His body. I'm so glad I anointed Him at table at Simon's house. I gave Him my precious Spikenard, the aroma filled the house, I will never forget. My hair smelled of it for days!

I couldn't sleep Friday night, nor Saturday. I collected herbs and oils. I determined I would go to Him at first light on the first day of the week.

As I hurried to the tomb with the other women, we worried about how we'd roll the stone away so we could get in, it was so big and heavy. Guards were there too, perhaps we could persuade them to help us?

When we arrived, the tomb was already open! We looked inside, Jesus was gone! The tomb was empty, what were we to do?

I rushed back to tell Peter and John. We all ran back, John got there first, and waited by the entrance peering in. Peter rushed up and went straight in! We saw the linen cloths lying there, and the head napkin folded separately. Someone had come and stolen Jesus.

I could stand no more. I went out into the garden, knelt down in the damp grass alone and wept bitterly, I was so sad.

How could this have happened? If only there was someone I could ask!

Oh there is someone near, the gardener has come to work early I expect. He speaks to me, "Woman, why do you weep? Whom do you seek?" My voice broke as I told him… then, Oh my… I heard my name spoken by a very familiar voice "Mary"... I just couldn't believe it! Jesus was as alive as ever, even though I'd seen His dead body laid in the tomb last Friday. This was the greatest miracle of all, and I was the first to witness it!

I couldn't wait to tell the others right now, this minute! I ran as fast as I could, breathlessly I burst into the room where they were all hiding. "I have seen the Lord," I cried out. The silence of disbelief met me. They thought I was living a fantasy, because I had loved Him so much, this was just my wishful thinking.

Later in the day, nearly all of us were together in the upper room. Only Thomas was missing. Two disciples who lived seven miles away in Emmaus came hurrying in, full of excitement with the amazing news that they had walked and talked with a stranger on their long walk home, who had turned out to be Jesus. They had recognized Him when He had broken bread. "Peace be with you"… a familiar voice filled the room.

There was the risen Jesus standing there among them.
Shirley

THINK ON THESE THINGS
You were born into a higher life of grace.

MARY ON EASTER MORNING
Nothing but the graveclothes. I could find nothing
else, as though, Lord, You were showing me
You were past the physical life, were where
eternal life was the only life that mattered.

I should have known, I should have hoped
the world's light would shine again at dawn.
And there was something more wonderful,
though at the time I couldn't see it.

The dear, dear life I couldn't touch or hold
and didn't recognize until you spoke, for
in one word, my name, Mary, I saw that
Resurrection life was personal and warm.

as was the presence of love for everyone
who knew You, as I knew You. and knew
You were the son of God, redeeming us.
And I saw that love had risen again

that we couldn't extinguish it, because it
was forever, with You, in the life to come, amen.
Selwyn

PRAYER
I glorify Your unending life that burst
triumphant from the rock, for on that
empty rock You built Your church,
and Your kingdom that has no end.

Rise up in my heart with Your great love
and roll away the stone that
shuts me from eternal life..
For You are risen from the dead.

And I understand why
we are blessed who mourned,
for now we are comforted
as You told us we would be.

Each Easter, when I bear the grief of looking at Your
cross, I understand why You are the Resurrection
and the Life that is eternal. For Your word is truth,
is forever truth, beyond my world's end.
Amen.

ON THE THIRD DAY

You triumphed over the shameful crucifix,
celebrated your Godhead and Your humanity,
were born again into a higher life of grace.

And I reflect how, in the stone-cold tomb,
you gathered new life, inhaled the fresh breath
of life we could not take from You again.

For we are blessed, who mourned
so much, for now we are comforted,
as You told us we would be.

You burst, triumphant, out of the rock, on which You'll
build Your church. Rise up in my heart with that great
love, and roll away the stone that blocks my path to You.

Lord, each Easter when You rise to life again,
leaving behind the dead; I understand anew
that You are my Redeemer, my Savior and my God.
Amen.
Selwyn

RESURRECTION

We thank you that Resurrection is not
simply a return to the old life
with its daily cares and concerns,
its shabbiness and its emptiness.

For resurrection life is new and abundant,
it is pure and faultless, it is the never-ending life,
lived close in the joy of Jesus our Lord,
and those we have long loved in our hearts.

For we are His for all eternity,
the peace of the Holy Spirit is over us,
and the great glory of God lies around us,
in the love of our one Redeemer and Savior,

Jesus Christ, our Lord, Amen.

The Road to Emmaus

RESURRECTION (2)
THE ROAD TO EMMAUS
BREATH OF HEAVEN, WAY OF HOPE

Were not our hearts burning within us while he was talking to us on the road, while he was opening the scriptures to us? (Luke 24:32)

Familiar roads are so delightful to travel. The seven-mile trek from Jerusalem to Emmaus must have been exhilarating as well as rugged terrain over hills and mountains. Cleopas and his unnamed companion most likely spoke often on this road concerning Jesus, their hope for a Messiah who would be a great military leader for their nation Israel. But today's journey was quite different, most unexpected. What an encounter! Nothing at all as these two disciples had planned. Their hearts were heavy as they began the trail. But a Stranger who joined them changed everything. What began as a hopeless walk ended in an unending vision of eternal hope. Let us join them in order to find out for ourselves how to turn our own roads into a breath from Heaven, a way of hope.

The 24th Chapter of the Gospel of Luke is packed with vital information concerning the tomb of Jesus, the road to Emmaus, the room where Jesus appeared to the disciple for the last time, and the short image of Jesus ascending into Heaven. There is much territory covered in this chapter and the story of the road to Emmaus is perhaps one of the most intriguing events in all the New Testament. Jesus has been crucified, laid in a tomb, and rose on the first day of the week. The two disciples had heard speculation about the events but decided to return to Emmaus in order to avoid being caught up in the danger that remained for the followers of Jesus. A Stranger joined them but scripture says that "their eyes were 'kept' from recognizing him." The two travelers were very, very sad. Their hopes were dashed. All that they had worked hard for, believed in, and given their entire beings to were dashed! Have you ever had such a journey? You gave all you had in a dream, worked night and day for its fulfillment, and kept on the path towards hope in the outcome only to be met with total disillusionment? Your road became an unrecognizable nightmare!

T.S. Eliot's revealing poem, *The Wasteland,* offers an image of that sense of total despair when life as we planned ends in what feels like destruction. Eliot describes the feeling as one of "frosty silence." So sad were the two disciples on the road to Emmaus that their eyes could not see the risen Jesus walking right beside them. They had always had a distorted vision of who Jesus was. His death destroyed their dream. But what they were kept from seeing was that whom they imagined Jesus to be was so much less than who he truly was. He was the God of the Universe who came to Earth for the salvation of all humanity. They wanted him just for Israel. They wanted a military leader. Jesus was a giver of eternal life. Jesus called them "foolish." He then even revealed to them through the writings of the Old Testament who the Messiah would be. Still, their eyes were blinded. Finally, they reached the end of the road and Jesus appeared to be walking on ahead when the two disciples invited him to stay over. As the three of them sat for a meal, something miraculous and mysterious happened. Jesus began to break bread. Suddenly, the scars on his nail-driven hands were revealed, and the manner in which he broke the bread exposed fully to the disciples who the Stranger was: it was the Christ whom they had loved and followed! Isn't it interesting how often God reveals himself to us in the smallest unexpected ways? Their eyes were opened and he vanished from their sight. Wow! What a trip this road to Emmaus had been for two despondent disciples. They got up and probably ran back to Jerusalem where they found the other disciples and joined them. While the two disciples were explaining what had happened on the road, Jesus appeared and stood among those gathered there. Even here Jesus kept on revealing who he was, let them see his scarred hands and feet, ate a bite of fish, and continued to give them instruction to stay because he was getting ready to do an even greater miracle. Jesus was sending them the Holy Spirit whom the Father had promised, and they would be clothed with power from on high. Then right after that promise, Jesus ascended into Heaven, making way for the Spirit to come and give them a supreme power that they had never known.

What an incredible story! When our roads are under significant reconstruction; when all of life as we have known it has been up shoveled and destroyed, there is new life on the horizon. Perhaps our eyes are temporarily kept

from seeing. Our ability to see new possibilities is distorted. Our hope is gone. We may even feel as T.S. Eliot expresses in his famous poem: "He who was living is now dead; we who are living are now dying…" But when the Stranger appears to us through faith, through the breaking of the bread, through his promise of power from on high, are we able to believe? Do our past limitations prevent our future reality? Are we able to believe that the Holy Spirit will soar with us to all that God has promised? Will we open our senses to the presence of the Spirit who is able to influence our whole beings by the calmness of his presence? Will we allow the Spirit to awaken within us dreams yet undreamed? Our road to Emmaus will end in hope, joy, love, and peace, and our future will no longer be built of false beliefs of the past. Now that we see Jesus fully and experience him as never before, our future will be bright with the hope of his revelation. Will you see Jesus breaking the bread in your heart? Amen.
Martha

THINK ON THESE THINGS
Walking familiar roads we often do not see You with us.

PRAYER
Dear Lord Jesus, we thank You that when
You had suffered and entered into Your glory,
You came to us at Emmaus and found us.

Our hearts burned within us as You talked
with us on the way, and the scriptures
overflowed with assured and certain light.

Renew in us that Emmaus gladness,
the sudden certainty when, quite unaware,
we welcome You into our homes and lives.

Draw near to us as we walk on the way,
appear to us plainly in Your risen presence
and let us follow You when You go to Jerusalem,

That we may share with Your disciples the
glorious reward of being in the room when
You first came back to them from the dead.

And we learn the great Emmaus lesson, that
You are so much more alive than we are.
And the new life You give will never end.
Amen.

Breakfast on the Beach

RESURRECTION (3)
BREAKFAST ON THE BEACH

The account is rich in examples of how wonderful is
our Savior, and how we should respond to Him and His
Father.

It was a surprise meeting from the start and perhaps the
most surprising thing, at any rate to the disciples, was the
fact that Jesus, their Lord and Creator was actually *waiting
for them.* He should have had no idea of where they were
going, but Jesus knows so much about us that we
shouldn't, really, be surprised at such unique foresight.

But in addition, Jesus leaves us free, even when He
might command us. For He respects our earthly ways and
weaknesses. He does not press us against our will. He
dispensed with His authority and was intent only on
meeting them again, face to face. He had done it so often
in the years of His ministry and we all remember old
acquaintances with pleasure. But perhaps He is often there,
waiting for us, also face to face, when our faith is weak
and we need His refreshment. We may not recognize Him,
as the disciples did not recognize Him, and this was true
also with the Emmaus disciples and even with Mary. But
He recognizes us. He doesn't pass by on the other side
because He knows how wounded we are and how much
we need His care.

We don't know as much as we would like about the
Resurrected Jesus, but we trust Him because He overflows

with care for our wellbeing. He had been at the beach before them, long enough to have prepared a breakfast. Because He knows our needs before we do and provides whatever we are lacking.

The custom of saying grace before a meal has widely fallen into disuse, largely, I suspect, because we do not acknowledge that our Lord is present, too. But we do not take a mouthful or a drink without His blessing us. We are no different from the disciples of old.

A beach on the sea of Tiberius seems an unlikely place to found His new church on earth, but this was what he did, later, with Peter. The incident with Peter is astonishing because he, Peter, had been naked in the boat, (however literally we take that), and had put on only an old coat, his father's, before jumping into the sea. And he had no opportunity to enhance his dress further before meeting his Lord. So Jesus set up his church and its leader on earth with a man wearing only his father's coat. It is true, of course, that our Lord had chided us for thinking too much about what we should wear. But I take leave to doubt that He intended things to go that far.

Nevertheless it is a real tribute to Jesus that he did not allow this or anything else to interfere in His purposes, which were far more important than Peter's dress. He charged Peter three times with feeding his sheep, so amongst other things, he would never forget. And if his memory faded or he grew cool, there were six other disciples there, hearing His words and ready to support

Peter in his work for Christ. They too had heard His words and received His great Commission.

So our Lord arranged things for His Church before He departed from this world.

The great catch was not purely symbolic.
Selwyn

THINK ON THESE THINGS
We must still go on feeding His sheep.

PRAYER
Jesus, who knows our natures and waits for us
when we are consumed with daily tasks,
set Yours plainly before us that we may work
for You and for Your kingdom here on earth.

We do not understand the love that tolerates so
much reluctance, so little response, that knows
us yet loves us as we are. But let us offer what
we are, for only You can free us from ourselves.

Surround me with Your holiness. Confront me with
Your sacrifice. Be the courage in my weakness and
my conviction when I talk of You. Uplift me to adore
Your goodness and Your comfort in the Holy Spirit.

So let us learn the tasks You set us, dear Jesus,

we would work only for You, hear only Your call
and when we turn, come unexpectedly across
your light and healing breaking into our lives.

So shall we respond to Your great love, and be
Yours for evermore, in Your kingdom of the forgiven.
Amen.

PENTECOST (1)

Perhaps I should first say what Pentecost means to me.

For me, Pentecost is the eternal breaking through into our lean and impoverished world. And the roots of Pentecost lie deep in prayer, since the scriptures tell us that it did not come until the disciples and the women had spent some 50 consecutive days in prayer. If ever proof were needed of the power of prayer, then surely it is in Pentecost that the evidence is most undeniable.

For they could not doubt their experience. The wind and the flames were beyond question. They were too immediate, too real, too powerful for doubt. And besides it left them with an irresistible need to communicate. A need that is still real and evident today. When something wonderful happens, when you find Jesus or fall in love, you have to tell someone, everyone, everything about it. And why should you want to keep something that wonderful to yourself? It would surely be contrary to the laws of nature.

They could not contain themselves. They immediately spoke to each other in tongues, then later that same day they spoke again, in public, and to great effect. For who can remain silent when they have welcomed Jesus into their hearts? Three thousand souls were converted that day, as a result.

For we are not talking of private prayer, excellent though that unquestionably is. Here, we are speaking of public prayer, shared with our brothers and sisters, expressing our

Pentecost

deepest needs and our personal commitments. Perhaps we should consider adjusting our prayers to be a little more like this. For it is worth remembering that all this happened after *public* prayer.

Though no doubt there was much private prayer as well. And let's not forget the apostles, they performed many signs and went from house to house celebrating the good news. For they knew that Pentecost is for everyone and for all time.

It is even for me. Amen.
Selwyn

THINK ON THESE THINGS
When the Holy Spirit comes, we cannot help speaking of the love of God in Jesus.

PRAYER
Holy Spirit You are here with us. Here in this room.
Forgive us when we do not see Your light
glowing all about us. For we are open
to You, to be marked, forever, from above.

So let us take Your pure and sacrificial love and bring it to the chill attention of the world, confront its harsh denials and tell how loving is the God of light, in whom there is no darkness at all.

In whom, alone, our salvation rests secure, to whom we look for our eternal life, our sins forgiven, in endless life with Him and with His son, our Lord and Savior Jesus Christ, Amen.

THINK ON THESE THINGS
Pentecost is a bursting dam and stream of living water.

REFLECTION
Pentecost is the first chord of a symphony. You cannot tell how it will grow.

PENTECOST (2)
PENTECOST: WIND, FIRE, AND DOVE

"And I will ask the Father, and he will give you another Advocate, to be with you forever" (John 14:15).

As this chapter is being written, it is Ascension Day in the year of the Church. Therefore, the celebration of the day that Jesus ascended back to heaven to sit at his Father's right hand has everything to do with Pentecost. Furthermore, Luke's Gospel tells us that Jesus instructed his disciples to return to Jerusalem and that they should remain in the city until they had been clothed with "power from on high." These things Jesus spoke to his followers within the timeline of the Jewish celebrations of Passover, when he was crucified, and Pentecost, the festival of Harvest. After the Resurrection of Jesus, he appeared to his disciples for forty days, continuing to teach and encouraging them to remain faithful. Ten days before Pentecost, Jesus ascended back to heaven. On the fiftieth day after Passover, the Father sent through his Son, Jesus, a miraculous power that changed each Person present forever. Approximately one hundred and twenty witnessed the power from on high and saw and heard things they had never experienced. Ultimately from that extraordinary power, three thousand people were brought into the new Church, which was created and formed through this miraculous Pentecostal event.

The Holy Spirit

Signs and symbols exist throughout the Old and New Testaments to enlighten the human mind's understanding of enormous spiritual realities far too deep to grasp. But, make no mistake about this phenomenon. The Holy Spirit is not a Dove. But he is rightly represented by the symbol of a Dove. Spirit as the third Person of the Holy Trinity, is every ounce as much a Person as the Father and the Son. At Pentecost, three significant symbols represented the power from heaven. Heaven came down to Earth in the outward symbols of wind, fire, and dove.

The Book of Acts gives us an image of tremendous and marvelous revelation. When the day of Pentecost had come, they were all together in one place. Then, suddenly from heaven came a sound like the rush of a violent wind, filling the entire house where they were sitting. Notice, just as at baptism when the Holy Spirit descended "like" a Dove, the wind was "like" the sound of a blast of a mighty wind. Fire, "like" the shape of a tongue, rested on each of them. Fire has always been a symbol of purging and cleansing. The form and sign of a "tongue" mean that those present would receive power to spread the Gospel to the world. The remaining forever presence of the Holy Spirit is easily represented by the symbol of a dove. So, the characters are given wind, fire, and a dove to comprehensively express the entire personality of the Holy Spirit at Pentecost. The wind and fire give an extreme sense of "power" and the dove as a revelation of the Holy Spirit's "quiet and remaining" power.

It is necessary to bring the following point to the phenomenon of Pentecost.

We are now living in the dispensation of the Holy Spirit, sent fifty days after the Feast of Passover. Pentecost actually in Greek means "fifty." The sending of the Holy Spirit at Pentecost correlated to the Jewish Feast of the Festival of "first fruits" of the wheat harvest established in Leviticus. This meant new beginnings, a potentially colossal harvest, and the beginning of a new dispensation, the birth of the Church, the Body of our Lord. The dispensation of the Father was that of the eternal Power of Creation. The dispensation of the Son was an era of the Father manifesting himself to humanity through a human being incarnate. This was the Advent of the Redeemer. God manifested himself through the voice of Jesus from without for humanity to experience his tremendous power. The Third Voice of the Holy Spirit was sent as the dispensation of God manifesting himself as the voice and strength from within. There is no more authoritative power than God within, communing intimately with every individual who will open their heart to this gift.

We remain at the present time in the dispensation of the Holy Spirit. The outcome is that the outward self-willed humanity disappears, and the inner union of the soul with God emerges as the power force so freely given at Pentecost. So may we each comprehend the gift of Pentecost. Within our hearts, like those who were present

when the Holy Spirit came from on high with power, may we be equipped to speak the Gospel of Truth to the entire world. Amen.
Martha

THINK ON THESE THINGS
Wind and flame of the Spirit, burn and blow in me.

PRAYER
Come to me in the breath of endless life.
Burn my weakness, blow away my doubts.

If ever prayer is Spirit led, it should be now,
when the day of Pentecost is fully come
and You are empowering me to speak
the name of my Savior, Jesus Christ.

Pour out Your Spirit on all who pray together.
Wind and flame of the Spirit breathe another
Pentecostal vision into my life. Release in me
Your holy energy that I may go out into the world

Speaking Your name, for on this day I witness
that God raised up my Savior, Jesus Christ.
Now Your tongues without words speak in my mind,
candle flames that light my way to You
Wind and flame of the Spirit burn and blow in me.

Come to me as the breath of endless life
In Jesus' name. Amen.

THE NICENE CREED
THE LORD AND GIVER OF LIFE

"As the scripture said, 'Out of the believer's heart shall flow rivers of living water.' Now he said this about the Spirit" (John 7:38-39).

"Through the gift of grace, which comes from the Holy Spirit, man enters into a 'new life,' is brought into the supernatural reality of the divine life itself, and becomes a 'dwelling place of the Holy Spirit,' a living temple of God." Pope John Paul 11

Every Sunday morning, Christians worldwide rise and pray together the beautiful words of the Nicene Creed. But unfortunately, these words can become rote and spoken in a monotonous tone. Yet, considering the tremendous faith and even great struggles that occurred in the early Church, it is so easy to bring them to pen and paper. These words define, clarify, and express in relatively few verses the tenets of the Christian faith, especially what Christians believe about the Holy Trinity.

The Nicene Creed accomplishes a definitive proclamation of the Person-hood of each member of the Trinity. Since scripture identifies the Father and Son without much variation in nomenclature, it is easy to understand who they are in relationship to each other. The Holy Spirit, however, for some people is a bit more difficult to understand. His names vary throughout Holy Scripture, sometimes Spirit of Truth, Spirit of God, and Spirit of Life, just to name a few.

Just as the Father is a Person and the Son is a Person, the Holy Spirit is also truly a Divine Person with whom the

The Nicene Creed

believer can form a potent relationship. Holy Spirit is often referred to with impersonal pronouns. He is also usually the Third Person in the rank of order. However, Spirit is no less important or less influential as a vital member of the Holy Trinity. And just as a follower of Jesus becomes the Friend of Christ and of the Father, the same follower becomes intimate friends with the Holy Spirit. The Creed specifies why this fantastic relationship with the Spirit is so dynamic: Holy Spirit is the Lord and giver of Life. The Incarnation is signified in the Creed as the work of the Spirit. The redemptive "overshadowing" of the Holy Spirit is responsible for the birth of the World's Savior. As a Person who loves, guides, protects, and teaches what is true, Spirit is sent to every believer at Baptism as "another helper." When we genuinely desire Spirit's presence, He will come to us as a gift, a gentle, loving, and respectful friend. He wishes to fill us with His own Spirit. Like all gifts, we must have an open heart to receive and appreciate Spirit as the breath of Life. As our own will decreases, the will of God increases with the presence of God's Spirit. The Creed also makes clear that it is the Holy Spirit who spoke through the Prophets. It is the Holy Spirit who also gives life and inspiration to us as we read Holy Scripture. The Holy Scriptures came into being through the inspiration and motivation of the Holy Spirit.

Ultimately, the Council of Nicaea 325 AD and Constantinople 381 AD drafted an incredible document. Thankfully this text has lasted through the ages to verify that Jesus Christ was Divine, eternally begotten by the

Father, and born of the Virgin Mary. The Council stated without question that this Son of God was of the same substance and essence as the Father. Although the Western and Eastern Churches disagreed over time about whence the Holy Spirit proceeded, both approved much of the Creed. Although they still differ today, neither deny that the Holy Spirit is a Person, a Divine Spirit, and the Third Person of the Holy Trinity. Both agree on the Spirit's extreme necessity and importance in the sanctification, spiritual growth, and miraculous presence desired by all who genuinely believe in a trinitarian Christian faith doctrine. Despite periods of debate throughout history, the Creed continues to communicate the essence of the Christian faith and the Love of God.

The Holy Spirit, without question, deepens our relationship with God unlimitedly. Spirit also brilliantly points to who the Son is and reveals Christ's redemptive work for our Salvation. The Spirit brings life to the body, heart, and soul. He heals and makes whole. Pope Benedict says that "it is for this reason… it is important that each one of us know the Spirit, establish a relationship with Him and allow ourselves to be guided by Him." Therefore, the Holy Trinity as One being shares an eternal existence of Divine Love. You and I are asked to join this everlasting feast of Love. Invited and bound to this Love through the Holy Spirit, we sit at the table of almighty God for all eternity. Amen.
Martha

THE NICENE CREED - AN APPRECIATION

God of amazing works whose sun lights our days and Your stars our nights, You came to me in Christ, light from heavenly light, though I crucified Him to wipe out my wicked deeds, but when He rose from His tomb on the third day, I knew He was my Savior and my God, alive in His Kingdom that will have no end. He will return to judge us all in mercy.

And I believe in the Holy Spirit, the Lord, the giver of Life, who comforts me and leads me into truth, and in Your church on earth. I confess my faults before You, I look for the Resurrection of the dead and the Life of the world to come. Amen.

Selwyn

THINK ON THESE THINGS

I believe (John 3:16).

PRAYER

I believe in God the Father who sings in my life
and in Jesus Christ, His only Son, risen and alive,
who came to earth and brought us the Father's love,

We crucified Him, though He was light from light,
but He rose again from the dead and will
come to judge us all in mercy.
And I believe in the Holy Spirit, the Lord and

giver of life, who challenges our apathy,
and fits us with power for His mission.
Let us offer in worship all that we are,
and all that, in Jesus, we may become
for Christ has touched us with salvation.

We praise and glorify our God, the three in one,
who came to us in Jesus, in whom I trust for
Resurrection and the life of the world to come.
Amen.

THE STONING OF STEPHEN

There is not a great deal I can say about St. Stephen, over and above the account in Acts, just three points in fact, which I understand is classic for a sermon, though this is not one.

Firstly, and very trivially, I assume that it is his feast day which is mentioned at the beginning of Good King Wenceslas, which I refer to only to show how highly, widely and justly he has been regarded. It makes the act of Good King Wenceslas and his page so appropriate to the time.

My second point is that we should not overlook (Acts 6.8) the fact that he performed miracles. Both our Lord and Peter told us that miracles were a form of approval by God. Our Lord even said that we should believe Him for the sake of the miracles, if for nothing else. And it was His works that He referred to as evidence when questioned by John's disciples. So miracles are very important. In short, Stephen wasn't just another martyr (unforgivable as that phrase undoubtedly is), nor was he only the first martyr, he was a martyr *approved by God.* He spoke irresistible words before the Council with the face of an angel. For he was, surely, soon to become one, himself.

And my third and final point rests on the almost incredible text (Acts 7:55) that he looked up into the open heavens and saw both the glory of God and Jesus.

It is difficult to overstate the enormous importance of that. *No other man on earth has seen God at any time,*

Saint Stephen

148

(though Moses got close). I can only see it as the ultimate measure of Stephen's greatness and the ultimate sign of God's approval. So I think it's worth pausing to think about what that involves in terms of his closeness to God. There seems to be no barrier between Stephen and his maker, and perhaps God is showing us his gratitude and His love for man He created the one man who remained true to His creation... I really don't know what words to use. It is difficult to resist the conclusion, (and I don't want to resist it anyway), that God loved Stephen deeply and overwhelmingly, as He would love us, too, if only we would forget our empty self-importance and let Him. It places Stephen in a category that I, at any rate, am unable fully to understand or express; a life with such close, unfettered access to God is virtually incomparable, even among saints. And I believe it was seeing that man could live this close to the love of God that critically converted Paul into one of Christ's greatest disciples for God wanted that, too. And it largely came to Paul through Stephen. Stephen is a figure who towers above other followers of Jesus, to his endless praise.

So this is not just a factual account of the first martyr's death, it is a new and compelling revelation of how close the Father and Jesus want to be to us all.

And we really can live our lives like that, If we faithfully and committedly have in us the mind that was in Christ Jesus.

Let us pray for a faith like St Stephen's. Amen.
Selwyn

THINK ON THESE THINGS
Lifted by grace, you saw your redeemer and your God.

PRAYER
You did not fear those who would kill your body
for you had filled it with the Holy Spirit,
spoke boldly before the men who would
stone you, put you mercilessly to death.

They killed you as you knew they would...
But, lifted by grace, you looked up and saw
what no one else on earth has seen,
your Savior and your God in sanctity.

Forgiveness never ends for it is cherished
deep in God's nature, and that can
never change. So, before you died
you prayed that they might be forgiven.

All praise be to you, St. Stephen. for
all your miracles, your faith and works,
and to all the saints and martyrs
here in earth and also in heaven.
Amen.

ON THE ROAD TO DAMASCUS
SAUL SEEKS OUT THE PEOPLE OF *THE WAY*

Stephen was a devout follower of Jesus. He was full of the Holy Spirit and through him many miracles and wonderful works were achieved in the Name of Christ. He spread the Good News of Jesus wherever he went.

This upset the leaders of the Synagogue. They arrested him and took him before the Sanhedrin. Lots of false charges were brought, and to the delight of the Synagogue leaders, the Sanhedrin condemned Stephen to death by stoning.

They dragged him out of the city, tore off their coats and laid them by a young man called Saul, who had joined in the angry crowd. He watched as the hurling rocks and stones slowly battered Stephen to death, and a cheer went up as he fell to the ground dead.

This affected Saul, and gave birth in him to a great hatred for all followers of Jesus. He determined there and then he would join in the persecution and wipe the name of Jesus right off the map.

He went from house to house in Jerusalem, dragging out men and women followers of 'The Way' as they called themselves, and imprisoning them. He loved this work, was so enthusiastic, he went to the High Priest and asked him to give him letters to the synagogues in Damascus, giving him authority to arrest and take any followers of The Way as prisoners to Jerusalem.

On the Road to Damascus

He gathered a group of men together, letters safely tucked away in his pocket, they set out on their mission to arrest and destroy the people of the Way and put an end to all this new teaching.

They were an enthusiastic little group, they chanted as they marched along

"We're on our way to arrest the people of The Way. Their way is no way. Ours is the only way."
Saul confided in one of the men that he'd had spies watching houses and reporting back to him what's been going on with particular Way people in Damascus. "I was told there's a man called Ananias; he's got influence. They say he's full of the Holy Spirit, whatever that is! He will be my first target. I know where he lives. I'll get him, just you wait and see! I'll drag him back to Jerusalem. That will put an end to all his nonsense. I can't wait to get there!" My spies have given me some addresses.

Suddenly Saul fell to the ground. The men with him heard a voice, "Saul ,Saul, why do you persecute me?" "Who are you?" Saul asked.

"I am Jesus whom you are persecuting," came the reply. Paul struggled to get up, he opened his eyes, but he could see nothing, only darkness.

"Please help me, I'm totally blind, I can't see a thing." They took him by the hand, and led him into the city to the home of a man called Judas. He lived on Straight Street. Saul stayed there, blind and in shock. He could neither eat nor drink, he was so stunned and scared.

News of Saul's expected arrival in Damascus spread

rapidly among the people of the Way. They decided to be particularly cautious.

Then Ananias saw a vision. The vision told him that Saul of Tarsus was praying, and that he too had had a vision, that a man named Ananias would come, heal him and restore his sight.

Ananias explained his fears to the Lord, but reluctantly, and with great trepidation he set out for Straight Street. Laying his hands on Saul, he said, "Brother Saul, the Lord Jesus, whom you met on the road, has sent me so that your sight may be restored, and you will be filled with the Holy Spirit."

Immediately the scales fell from his eyes, he was baptized, and after eating, so full of the Holy Spirit was Saul, he preached and convinced people that Jesus was The Christ.

So successful was he that the jews planned to kill him. What a turnaround! The Damascus Christians helped him to escape in a basket through a hole in the city walls. Such an amazing event was this! God saw the potential in Saul, but the Way followers had to listen, trust, and obey the Holy Spirit's promptings.

It's a thought, but if Ananias had said "No," we may never have heard of Jesus. Saul, who became St. Paul. traveled widely and wrote extensively… but that's a story for another day!

I ask myself, is my faith and trust strong enough to put myself in danger for the sake of Jesus?
Shirley

THINK ON THESE THINGS
Marked from above.

PRAYER
Thank you, Lord, for giving us St. Paul,
marked from above. For though he left Jerusalem
breathing slaughter against all Christians

in Damascus, on the way he met the Lord,
was blinded by his closeness to the
invisible Jesus, light from heavenly light.
full of immortal power.

You lay three days in Damascus, in the darkness,
without food or water, were you reflecting how our Lord
had lain in the tomb, like that, awaiting new life.

And we thank the Lord that your reverence for your
Savior knew no bounds, for you had received
the truth, not from man, but from God in Jesus Christ.

You gave your life for Jesus, as He had given
His life for you, and closely identified with Him,
Saying, "I have been crucified with Christ."

You became the apostle to the Gentiles, and
took great missionary journeys, bringing them
to our Gentile hearts where they will live forever.
Amen.

Christ in Glory

CHRIST WILL COME AGAIN IN GLORY

Christ will come again in glory and we shall rejoice and be glad. But I do not expect it to be the glory of the world.. He will come in the glory of innocence and in the majesty of pain endured and Resurrection life. And so ,many will welcome Him. Those whose mourning is deep, but whose mourning fades at His approach; the poor in spirit and those who are persecuted and falsely reviled, for they know that now their case will be justly heard. Their joy is complete as He comes for they know they are loved in spite of everything. His enemies are glad. They know He loves them too.

So, He will come in His sacredness, and in His purity, and we shall rejoice to receive our Savior amongst us again. For most of all He restores us to the loving heart of God the Father and offers us again innocence such as we had so long ago, when He created us in His own image without fault and loving. Before we fell.

We fell. But it is among the most fundamental and significant things I believe that we can all be changed by a great love. So come, let us turn again to the God who is our Father, through the great love of His Son, and let us hold to Him, because there is no other hope but His love. And there is no other healing for our souls but in His infinite goodness.

For His ways are wonderful and His laws are laws of righteousness and care. He lives by them, Himself. For

He is the God who heals our brokenness, and the God who calls us in love.

Of course we shall remember His suffering and death. But His pain is part of His glory, too. As His grief and sorrow are part of the abuse we laid on Him in His life on earth. So surely it would be only right if we are praying when He comes.

It must have been profoundly difficult to know the mind of God and live with the grossness of humanity. Yet He did both. We failed to do it, abjectly, when You came to us You were always reproving Your disciples for their lack of faith, they failed time and again the test of belief in Your divinity, and too often it showed.

But we do not have to wait to see that glory spread before us. We may come to Him before He comes to us at the world's end. For He, Himself, has taught us how to pray, and in our prayers we meet Him, closely, warmly in total forgiveness, in brotherhood and sisterhood for all. We each find different ways to worship Him but He welcomes all our worship, no matter how lowly that worship may be. For it is our devotion that matters to Him. It is all that ever has.

And there is no better way for the world to end than in our heartfelt prayers, and in the joy of hymns sung to the everlasting glory of our eternal God and King. So come let us worship and bow down, let us kneel before the Lord, our maker. For He will come to us again. And we shall rejoice and be glad in Him. Forever. Amen.
Selwyn

THINK ON THESE THINGS
Our faithful song brings Him joy.

PRAYER
Lord who in all things shows Your love for us
sustain and keep us in Your holiness,
For You offer us life that is forever,
when we rise to Your eternal kingdom.

Inspire me with your grace that I may seek
only that which endures beyond the passing
of the earth, for we are no longer ordinary
people who live by your mercy and in the Spirit .

Walk with me in the cool of the evening,
in the garden, that Your Holy Spirit may
lead me from darkness into light. May that
mind be in me that was in Christ Jesus that
I may love the things of holiness and light..

Lord, who keeps me in Your care, nourish me in
prayer and raise me up as day succeeds each day.
We thank you that good is eternal and will triumph
over wrong in the eternal life of Your Kingdom.

So we look for Your coming in the glory
of our redeemer to judge us in mercy and love, Amen.

The Holy Spirit

THE HOLY SPIRIT: BREATH OF GOD

"The mouth of God is the Holy Spirit, and God's Word is his Son, also God."

Simeon the New Theologian (949-1022 AD)

A Sacred Presence in the Life and Work of Jesus has been an exhilarating process and a genuine revelation concerning the extraordinary importance of the Holy Spirit's sustaining and remaining presence in Jesus' divine accomplishments. The Holy Spirit is omnipresent from the outset of Jesus' ministry to the closing of his ministry. Just as Holy Spirit is present in Creation, hovering over the void and creating not only order but also breathing Life into mankind, so too, in the work of Jesus, he is omnipresent. As the third person of the Holy Trinity, Holy Spirit is "the mouth of God." He is a Person, not a symbol. The Son of God, also God, came to Earth Incarnate through the Power of the Holy Spirit. This Word, Jesus, spoke Truth by the Holy Spirit concerning the love of the Father for all Creation, especially humankind.

The function of the Holy Spirit in the believer's life is staggering. He is the Lord and Giver of Life. As the breath of the living God, the Holy Spirit's function is to offer all who come to him fresh strength and renewal. He is the living water promised to us who believe and the fountain of Life. Here are just a few roles the Holy Spirit performs in the lives of those who believe:

1) Sculpts the image of Jesus into our human nature, even bringing us into participation in the divine nature of Christ.

2) A helper who teaches

3) He convicts the world of Sin

4) He is the source of revelation, wisdom, and power

5) Gives Spiritual Gifts and beautiful fruit

6) Seals us in Baptism and is a down-payment for our inheritance in all hope for what the Gospel promises

7) Intercedes for our needs and helps us with our weaknesses

8) Gives us Eternal Life

9) Sanctifies us and makes us Holy. He inspires us, interprets Scripture, and is responsible for God's inspired Word.

These are only a few critical points about our need for the Holy Spirit. And just as the Holy Spirit raised Jesus from the dead, we, too, have that hope in the life to come.

We have seen how the Holy Spirit empowered Jesus in his Life and work. We have also seen how the Holy Spirit came at Pentecost to authorize the Church with Power from on high to carry the Gospel to the whole ends of the Earth. We are honored and blessed to be living in that same dispensation of the work of the Holy Spirit and the Church.

The Holy Spirit is a gift from Heaven who must be an "invited" Guest. Luke's Gospel tells us that the Father, through the Son, will give the Holy Spirit to those who ask. If we genuinely wish to know God, we must ask for the Holy Spirit to teach us everything. Like the Apostles at Pentecost, we will be empowered to change the world. The Power from on High will give us all we need to be transformed and to help others into the joy of New Life.

Since the Holy Spirit is the bond of love proceeding from the love of the Father and Son, we will be caught up in this feast of love. Knowing the Holy Spirit means fully experiencing and knowing who we really are.

Simeon, the New Theologian, summarizes Life in the Spirit in the following words: "The aim of all those who live in God is to please our Lord Jesus Christ and become reconciled to God the Father by receiving the Holy Spirit...every path of life which does not lead to this is without profit." May we ask ourselves this question: have I deeply desired to know the Holy Spirit above all else in Life? To know Him is to have abundant, joyful, and fruitful Life. May it be so for all who read these words. Amen.

Martha

Sacred Presence

THE HOLY SPIRIT
LIFE WITHOUT END

"...who brought you good news by the Holy Spirit sent from heaven--things into which angels long to look." 1 Peter 1:12

Throw wide the gate of your heart, stand before the sun of the everlasting light. St. Ambrose

What glorious good news that our Salvation through Jesus Christ brings to us through the Holy Spirit. One hymn describes this glory: "Holy, Holy, Holy is what the angels sing, but they never felt the joy that our salvation brings." The angels do not know what it means to overcome the power of evil, fight the battle of sin, and be transformed into Christ's image through the power of the Holy Spirit. Only flawed and fragile human beings have this eternal privilege. Through the Holy Spirit, the Lord and Giver of Life, what endless good news it is to know that our destiny can be with each other, the angels, saints, Jesus, the Father, and the Holy Spirit shouting "Holy, Holy, Holy." Can you imagine in heaven, the angels touching you on the elbow and saying, "When you have a moment, would you please tell us what it was like to be steeped in sin and rescued by the power of the Blood of Christ, and empowered to become saints through the power of the Holy Spirit?"

We have come to the end of our book, but we are just now beginning the road to our eternal purpose in the Lord Jesus Christ, vested and led by the power of the Holy Spirit. Through the power of the Holy Spirit, we will be changed from glory unto glory! There is never an end to the unfolding of our real being when centered in His Sacred Presence. By remaining in His sublime presence, we gain daily all we need to overcome that evil spirit that desires our downfall, and who rejoices when we are in a state of confusion and despair. True eternal joy rests in the presence of the Holy Spirit.

The state of Sacred Presence is not automatic. This state of grace requires something of ourselves also. God has given us all we need to be saved, yet He desires our will to be aligned with His Will. Basil of Caesarea describes this state of presence so beautifully: "The Spirit, like the sun falling on the purest eyes, will show us in himself the image of the invisible." This statement may explain why remaining in "Sacred Presence" is difficult. Humans need the comfort of visibility; we need to touch, feel, taste, see, and smell. Holy Spirit is invisible and requires pure faith. The Image of the Invisible adequately describes what is required of each person who longs to be made into the image of Christ. It is precisely the Sacred Presence of the Holy Spirit, the invisible third Person of the Holy Trinity who has the power and anointing to bring us safely home to our Father in heaven.

Thank you for joining us in our journey to explore who this Sacred Presence is, this glorious friend given to us from on high. We pray that you have experienced the magnitude of this precious and rare gift with us. While we have barely scratched the surface of the vastness of this subject, one thing we can clearly conclude: The Sacred

Presence is available to all whose eyes like the sun are willing to perceive the image of the invisible. Amen.

Martha

THINK ON THESE THINGS
In your state of grace, we live forgiven, and look to share Your grace in the power of the Holy Spirit.

PRAYER
You come to us in our every need
and greet us in the gentleness of the meek.
We rejoiced and You were glad with us, we wronged You
and You came quickly to forgive us.

We thank You for life and for freedom,
we give You every glory for we worship You
with the wonder of the forgiven.

We shall be persecuted, but we shall not waver,
for You, too, were rejected on earth.
So we shall forever adore You
in Your Kingdom of eternal love, Amen.

A PARTING PRAYER

Dear Lord, You have given us everything we have
we owe you our very lives.
And we praise You that You offer us life that is forever,
that as we pass from this life with all Your blessings
rich upon our heads, we pass to even greater blessings,
to share with You for all the years of eternal life.
Amen.

Shirley, Selwyn, and Martha each offer you their warmest
blessings.

ABOUT THE AUTHORS

Shirley Veater is Selwyn's wife, a daughter of The Manse. Studied art at Southlands College, London, and Brighton University.

She has always had a great love of painting, has had pictures accepted by the Royal Academy of Art in London. She had a 'one woman' retrospective Exhibition in Brighton.

Many of her larger works hang in Churches who have commissioned her. Also her work has appeared in a great many exhibitions.

Shirley says, "I find my work is a useful outreach tool, for as we talk about the painting, we are actually focusing on Jesus and talking about Him."

Selwyn Veater was born in Wales. He achieved an honours degree in Philosophy at the University of Wales in Cardiff. Sadly, he was unable to apply to continue to Oxford University, as at 16, his father died. He joined the Civil Service, became a Controller, then an Assistant Director in the Post Office.

He is a published, award-winning poet with works in many prestigious publications.

He is a devout Christian.

Selwyn believes: "imagination is the essence of art forms."

The Rev. Dr. Martha Toney is a native of Spartanburg, South Carolina. She is an ordained Deacon in the Episcopal Diocese of Central Florida. Martha's early life was spent as a professional opera singer, both in New York City and eleven years in Hof Theatre, Hof, Germany. Dr. Toney holds a Doctor of

Ministry in Theological and Biblical Studies from the Graduate Theological Foundation, as well as a Master of Ministry from Southern Wesleyan University and a Master of Music from the Manhattan School of Music.

Martha is a board-Certified Chaplain, holding 6 units of Clinical Pastoral Education. She was also personally trained by John Maxwell as a certified public speaker.

Martha also authored and published *Journey to Living Light* and *Journey to Daybreak*.

GROUP STUDY QUESTIONS
ON THE HOLY SPIRIT

1. The Nicene Creed states that the Holy Spirit is the Lord and giver of life. Discuss how this theme is also mentioned in the Old Testament. Genesis 2:7; Job 33:4.

2. What is the aim and purpose of the Holy Spirit being sent to the believer? Ephesians 3:16-18.

3. What does Scripture say about the Spirit as the power through which Jesus began his Galilean Ministry? Luke 4:14.

4. If the Holy Spirit raised Jesus from the dead, how does the Spirit renew, empower, and strengthen us in difficult periods of our lives? 1 Corinthians 15; Romans 8:11; Galatians 1:1.

5. What does Jesus say about the Holy Spirit dwelling inside his followers? John 14:17.

6. What does Jesus mean when he says that the Spirit teaches us and brings all that Jesus said to our memory? John 14:26.

7. How do we know that the Holy Spirit is a person and not a thing? John 14:26.

8. Why did Jesus need to leave before He could send the Holy Spirit? John 16:7.

9. What does Jesus say about the role of the Holy Spirit in sin, righteousness, and judgment? John 16:6-11.

10. Why does Jesus say he could not reveal everything to the disciples while with them? John 16:12-15.

11. How does the Holy Spirit intercede for us? Romans 8:26.

12. How does the Spirit know what we need and how to teach the will of God? Romans 8:27.

13. How does life in the Spirit set us free from the law of sin and death? Romans 8:1.

14. Can the Holy Spirit be grieved? Ephesians 4:30.

15. How does the Holy Spirit search all things? 1 Corinthians 2:10 and Jeremiah 17:10.

16. What role does the Holy Spirit have in sanctifying grace, renewing our spirits, and refreshing us to be effective witnesses for Christ? Acts 1:8; 2 Thessalonians 2:13-14.

17. How does the Holy Spirit bring peace and eliminate confusion? 1 Corinthians 14:33.

18. What does Holy Scripture say about the Holy Spirit's role in the revelation of God's Word? 2 Timothy 3:16.

19. Discuss this quote from St. Athanasius: "…all goodness descends from the Father, through the Son, and it reaches us in the Holy Spirit."

20. What does Peter mean when he speaks of human will and prophecy of scripture? 2 Peter 1:21.

21. How does the Holy Spirit bring the written Word of God to life? 1 Corinthians 2:11.

22. Discuss this quote from St. Gregory of Nazianzus: "There is no other way of knowing God for you except to live in Him."

23. How does the Holy Spirit help God to live in us? What are the Fruit of the Spirit? Galatians 5:22-26.

24. Discuss how the aim of our Christian life involves having the Holy Spirit indwell us?

25. Why does the book of Revelation begin and end with the Holy Spirit? Revelation 1:4; Revelation 22:17.

26. How can you use this study to encourage believers to know the *power of God who* raised Jesus from the dead?

27. Discuss the Trinity and how the sacred presence of the Holy Spirit inside of us after Pentecost changed the boldness of His disciples. Acts 1-3

28. Discuss the term *pure faith*, and how we demonstrate our faith to unbelievers.

29. Discuss the baptism (John the Baptist) with water and the infilling baptism (with fire) by the Holy Spirit.

30. How can we live so not to grieve the Holy Spirit?

31. How has this book led you to a greater understanding of the Holy Spirit in your walk with Christ?

Made in the USA
Monee, IL
05 October 2023